M000187458

"No matter how ︙ ·taking. We think that forn. ......, --- ---y ---... --g us down with their demands or lead to discouragement when they fail to deliver. In *Child Proof*, Julie Lowe helps us rethink parenting so that in faith, we can love our children personally and minister God's wisdom to their unique needs."

Brian Liechty, Pastor for Care & Counseling, Bethlehem Baptist Church North Campus

"When you have prayed for your kids, sought to lovingly encourage them with Jesus, and things are still a mess, Julie comes along at just the right moment with creative suggestions that give fresh direction."

Ed Welch, Faculty and Counselor, CCEF; author of *A Small Book about a Big Problem*

"Julie's home is a 'story.' That's her word. It's what God has been writing in her, her husband, and their six kids. Each chapter of their parenting story emerges in the chapters of *Child Proof* to show other imperfect parents how Christ, by faith, is sufficient for their story with their unique children. *Child Proof* is biblically principled, realistically wise, immediately applicable, and filled with hope."

Rick Horne, Author of *Get Outta My Face! How to Reach Angry, Unmotivated Teens with Biblical Counsel* and *Get Offa My Case! Godly Parenting of an Angry Teen*

"Simplistic and cookie-cutter approaches to parenting overpromise and underdeliver. Julie Lowe offers a parenting pathway that is far wiser and richer. She shows that loving our children is a multifaceted venture of faith-filled dependence on God, patient and careful study of our children, and creative application of biblical wisdom to the particularities of each child's life."

Michael R. Emlet, Faculty and Counselor, CCEF; author of *CrossTalk: Where Life and Scripture Meet* and *Descriptions and Prescriptions: A Biblical Perspective on Psychiatric Diagnoses & Medications*

"How can we parent with wisdom and grace in a rapidly changing world that offers increased parenting challenges and parenting formulas that may *seem* right but which fail to deliver? With vulnerability and experience, Julie Lowe offers practical, biblically sound guidance on how to parent faithfully—recognizing that God can and will work in us and through us as we face parenting challenges, fears, and difficulties. In a day and age marked by the collapse of parenting, Julie will help you to pause, ponder, and regroup in ways that will better equip you to parent to the glory of God."

Walt Mueller, President, Center for Parent/Youth Understanding

"I wish this book had been available when I was raising my kids! No formulas. No 'ideal families.' But hope and help for *real* parents, *real* children, *real* conversations, *real* life, with a *real* God. It presents a high call to love our kids with Jesus's sacrificial, personalized love and the freedom to let go of trying to manipulate the results. I hope every current and prospective parent will read this book!"

Elizabeth W D Groves, Lecturer in Biblical Hebrew, Westminster Seminary; author of *Grief Undone: A Journey with God and Cancer*

"In this social media age we are programmed to look for 'five steps to this' and 'three reasons for that.' Sometimes this approach can be helpful but it's often too simplistic to address complex issues such as family life and parenting. Formulas can be even more exasperating when they ignore the individual aptitudes, personalities, and needs of our children. What is most impressive about this book is that it resists the pressure to come up with formulas for parenting, and instead, provides biblically grounded tools and practical wisdom to help the reader with one of the greatest challenges anyone has to face: being a parent."

Timothy Witmer, Emeritus Professor of Practical Theology, Westminster Theological Seminary; author of *The Shepherd Leader at Home*

"For anyone who has secretly suspected that the typical parenting formulas can't cope with the complexity of your family life, this book will be a revelation. With her typical warmth, wit, and biblically rich wisdom, Julie has blown the roof off my tightly held, false parenting expectations. Instead, with realism and honesty, she points the way to parenting by faith in the Lord who is present even in the most complex of family moments. I have never read a parenting book that left me more hopeful."

Ste Casey, Course tutor and speaker, Biblical Counselling UK; pastor, Speke Baptist Church, Liverpool, UK

CHILD PROOF

PARENTING BY FAITH, NOT FORMULA

Julie Lowe

New
Growth
Press

WWW.NEWGROWTHPRESS.COM

New Growth Press, Greensboro, NC 27404
www.newgrowthpress.com
Copyright © 2018 by Julie Lowe

Cover Design: Faceout Books, faceoutstudio.com
Interior Typesetting and eBook: Lisa Parnell, lparnell.com

ISBN: 978-1-948130-15-8 (Print)
ISBN: 978-1-948130-16-5 (eBook)

Library of Congress Cataloging-in-Publication Data on file

Printed in the United States of America

25 24 23 22 21 20 19 18   1 2 3 4 5

Dedication

To my family. You have inspired me to strive
to be a more Christlike wife, mother, and individual.
You are my peeps, my tribe, my posse, and I love you.
May this book be a reflection of the many ways
the Lord has worked in our home and our stories.

Contents

Foreword
by David Powlison

Consider the way in which our Lord parents his children. He is setting out to create an ever-deepening, lifelong friendship. He treats each of us with a personalized touch. He initiates and sustains an honest conversation about consequential matters. Our God comes as a compassionate father, and he is even more attentive than a nursing mother. He knows his children, knows their gifts, knows their limitations, knows their sins, knows their graces. He's a patient parent. It's safe to depend on him. He freely tells us he has plans for our good, a future of peace and hope. We can trust his care. He freely tells us his will for us. All that he does and says works to teach us how to love from a pure heart, a good conscience, and a sincere faith. He wills that we become truly good parents from the heart, like him. He loves us wisely.[1]

It's an inspiring picture. But it's easy for us to try to take his self-revelation a step further and expect that he will also give us a formula for how to live it out. We want a to-do list, a defined program with specific action steps. But God doesn't give a to-do list for raising a family. There are too many variables. And he never guarantees that if you just do *ABC* with your children, eventually they will turn out *XYZ*.

---

1. Here are some of the Scriptures that fill out this paragraph: Psalm 25:14; Psalm 103:13–14; Isaiah 49:15–16; Jeremiah 29:11; 1 Timothy 1:5.

Most books on raising children try to give you the formula. They're a bit like diet plans. They sort of work for some people for a while. But they always disappoint in the end. Books on child-rearing often offer some good ideas, even very good ideas. But you discover you're not wired quite like that author, and your kids aren't wired like those kids, and their life situation isn't the same as your life situations. Whatever your good intentions, you can't do life in the same way the child-rearing book says you should.

Even more fundamental, the premise is wrong. Wise parenting always has a dynamic, improvising quality. Child-rearing is not like computer programming or car mechanics. It's an action adventure. When you're in the middle of it, you never know what's coming around the next corner. The things you most need to know can't be summarized on a to-do list, can't be programmed. That's exactly the way God intends life to work—so we always *really* need him.

Julie Lowe gets the premise right. She gives you a way of coming at the whole adventure of being a parent. Yes, she offers some good ideas along the way, some very good ideas. But more than that, she will invite you to live in a way that opens the door to loving a child in the ways this particular child needs to be loved.

Acknowledgments

I can say with utter certainty that this book would not have been written without the encouragement of my colleagues at CCEF. Second only to my family, they have sharpened me personally and professionally, and taught me much about understanding people.

Equally, I could not have done this without New Growth's Barbara Juliani guiding me, encouraging me, and assuring me that I had something helpful to say. She is a major reason that this manuscript exists. Thank you for your commitment to steering me through the process. I am grateful for the skillful editing of Barbara Juliani and Sue Lutz. It brought me great comfort to know that you both were a part of the process.

When God Writes Your Story

At a meeting with my editor, I was holding a mug of coffee (essential to daily life) that read, "I childproofed the house, but they keep getting in." We laughed about that—she has four children and I have six—but our laughter was rueful. Because the truth is that we do want to childproof our homes. Not to keep our children out, but to make sure that once and for all they remain safe. It's what all parents want, right? Safety and a guaranteed good outcome. We want that so much that we are easily persuaded to reach for a parenting formula or recipe—Do this! Don't do that!—that promises to "childproof" our homes. But parenting formulas not only don't deliver the promised outcome (safe, happy, never-in-trouble kids), they keep us from parenting by faith. So we miss out on a rich life of trusting God to guide us in knowing and loving our children and guiding them toward love for God and others in ways that are specific to their unique gifts and needs.

The theme of this book—parenting by faith and wisdom, not formula—is born out of both personal and professional experience. As a counselor, I've met with many families seeking help with parenting questions or struggles their child was facing. Often parents wanted an immediate solution, when what they really needed was *time* to learn how to understand their children and what motivated their behavior. They needed time to examine both the problem and their own responses to it as parents. They needed time to discern what godly parenting responses looked like in that particular situation. Once in a while, there was a clear solution that could be implemented immediately, but it was rare for me to be able to offer parents a magic bullet or quick fix.

Most of the time, when it comes to marriage and family life, it takes time to build trusting relationships, to know each other well, to know ourselves well, and to develop biblical insight that enables us to speak wisely and lovingly into another person's life. But when we take the time to learn how to do this, and strive to love God and to love others with his love, we discover that God gives us tremendous liberty to express that love in ways that are distinctive to our situation. God does not limit us; he liberates us to godly self-expression in the way we establish our home.

My husband, Greg, and I married in our thirties. Before that, I had become a foster parent to two little girls, sisters ages two and three. As a single person, I'd had a deep desire to foster children and eventually adopt. As a counselor and social worker, I was aware of the challenges involved and I wanted to think wisely about taking on that responsibility as a single person. Was it biblical, wise, and even "right" to do so? I encountered some strong opinions, some from people who thought it unwise. I had to think carefully about doing life in an unconventional way and ask if it could still be pleasing to God. If I never married, would I be able to live out my personal convictions? What did biblical wisdom look like in this instance?

When Greg and I married, our two little foster girls walked down the aisle ahead of us as flower girls. Right before the wedding, we'd found out that we would be able to adopt the girls, and our wedding became a celebration of God bringing us together as a family. I was given a new last name and so were the girls. The girls were given a mom and dad, and Greg and I were given children. As then three-year-old Brittney reminded me, "God knew you needed kids." Within a few months, Greg and I were asked to consider adopting two little biological brothers. Within the first year of marriage, we found ourselves with four children under the age of five.

Those decisions came with many implications for our parenting. I was both mom and dad for a season. Greg and I both had to work within a foster care system with its rules and regulations. We had to accept regulations on how we could and could not parent, and build relationships with birth parents. We had to think creatively and wisely about how we would address behavior issues and consequences, and how we would help our kids make sense of hard experiences they'd had early on.

We have since added two more children to our family, along with a menagerie of pets. It's a full life. Many of our kids are now teenagers and we continue to serve as foster parents. Early on, we adopted the posture that God would build our family as he saw fit. Whether we were given biological, adopted, or foster children, whether we had kids for a season or permanently, we would trust God to bring the children he wanted to our home. We would also trust him for wisdom about when to say yes or no. We have had children come and go. We have had heartache and loss, kids with challenging behaviors and circumstances, disabilities, and brokenness. Greg and I have had our own struggles, temptations, and parenting challenges. All of these things have made us lean on the Lord more, as we have asked him to help us understand what Scripture has to say to us, and asked the Holy Spirit to help us apply it to our family.

In a very good way, our family has required us to approach Scripture, the gospel, and conventional parenting ideals by asking, "How does this apply to our home and our circumstances?" This also has become a theme in my counseling. I have seen families heal and prosper as parents sought to understand their kids and to see how Scripture applied to the uniqueness of their marriages, families, and home life.

In our family and in families I've counseled, we have seen both our freedom and our great responsibility to know each child well and parent them with wisdom. We strive to know our children individually, and prayerfully ask what it looks like to love each one, to speak into their lives, and to make decisions that benefit them. We do not always get it right, but when we focus more on parenting wisely and faithfully, we can trust God with the outcome. Our goal is not success (at least as the world defines it). It is faithfulness in our task.

We've been persuaded to stop being ruled by potential outcomes or what others thought or did in their homes. Instead we seek to rely on the Lord to equip us. Our understanding of parenting by faith requires us to accept failure, suffering, potential risks, and disappointments. We don't pursue the promise of success or a perfect family. This liberates us to simply follow the Lord and focus on the needs of our home. Without a doubt, this requires far more effort, time, and discernment, but it also gives tremendous freedom to *not* look for formulas or mimic other families. We have the freedom to establish our marriage and home life—its structures, rules, and roles—based on our needs and the God-created individuality within our family. Our home is not an example of the ideal family, nor do we want to be. It is the story of us, the story God is writing. We embrace both its blessings and brokenness. We hope to faithfully walk in the story God has given us, and faithfully steward the lives of our children and the stories he is writing for them.

A family is always a work in progress. With time, developmental changes, and new seasons of life, we will always have the freedom and responsibility to adapt. We have a faithful God who is writing each of our stories. Every one is different, with different characters, circumstances, lessons, blessings, sufferings, twists, and turns. He can write a better family story than you or I could ever imagine. He will take the blessings and sufferings of each unruly character and weave them together in an amazing narrative of redemption and love. We may not know what the next chapter holds, but we do not need to be discouraged by the details of the story. It is still being written. The Author of the story is good and he can be trusted implicitly.

What does Scripture have to say about my child's struggles, my parental fears, or our unique circumstances? A great deal! Biblical wisdom wrestles with bringing Scripture to life in our particular stories. Will you trust him with your story? With your children's stories? Will you allow him creative liberty in each chapter you face? Will you seek him with all your heart and seek to love your family as Christ loved the church? If so, you will find great liberty to live family life—not perfectly, but wisely.

Part I

THE FOUNDATIONS
FOR PARENTING BY FAITH

CHAPTER 1

Freedom vs. Formula

Bill and Amanda are the parents of three children: Matthew (age 4), Rachel (age 6), and Micah (age 14). They are both working parents, involved in church, and trying their best to juggle the business of life and family activities. Like many parents, they are looking for solutions to the problems that their children are experiencing. Micah is consumed with his phone and seems to be slowly withdrawing from family life. Rachel is anxious and struggles just to get on the morning bus, and Matthew is a typical high-energy child who wears his mother out with his constant movement.

Bill and Amanda came for counseling to find out what they could do to make their family "function normally." As we talked together about what "normal function" meant to them, we realized that they were looking for "*the* thing" they could do so that their kids would obey, not struggle, and be happy, decent young people. Surely, there is *a* right thing, a foolproof recipe for producing the results they are looking for?

I get it. I am like this with my children too. I want a formula for successful parenting. I want a parenting roadmap with directions (like my GPS) that tell me where to turn. And I definitely want the guarantee that my family will end up at the right destination. I don't want to have to struggle or wonder; just tell me the next step and I will take it.

Many parents are avid readers. I know I am. I want to get better at parenting, and reading a parenting book by an expert seems like a great way to get the family GPS I'm looking for. But I often struggle to apply what I have read to my own family and to the parenting my husband and I do. I notice in myself and in the parents I counsel the tendency to take what we read or hear and try to craft a one-size-fits-all approach to our children: do these things and your family will function well. But all too often, we feel defeated, frustrated, and stuck when it seems that we've followed the rules, yet our children still struggle, appear unresponsive, and/or have challenging behaviors.

At that point, we can feel abandoned by God, discouraged, and frustrated. From there, it's easy to simply revert to our own ways, ways that seem right and natural to us. We move toward a parental pragmatism that justifies our bad reactions, our passivity, and a paralyzing defeatism. What we fail to see during those times is that we have *not* been abandoned by God as we have attempted to parent. The reality is that biblical truth and biblical principles are *always* at work and always offer hope and help. They remain true and effective even when we feel that our children are not responsive.

The place where we flounder is in our application of these biblical principles. We want someone to give us ten steps to apply the Bible to our family life, and we want it to work NOW! But that is not how it works. Applying biblical principles and truth to your specific family (and mine) also requires biblical wisdom, the kind of wisdom that comes from God and is gentle, peaceable, full of mercy, and good fruit. From that wisdom we are promised a harvest of righteousness that brings peace (James 3:17–18). But it doesn't come through a formula.

How *do* we grow in biblical wisdom? It starts with knowing and loving God, and going to him for what we lack. God promises to give wisdom to those who seek it (James 1:5), and the wisdom he gives is tailor-made for our children and for us. It's a practical expression of what it means to love God and love others. The thing to remember is that, while the biblical princi-ples remain universal and unchanging, the way they are *applied* in specific ways is unique to each family's personalities, gifts, difficulties, and circumstances. The way God has structured it, there is much more liberty in how we live out godly principles in marriage and family life than we often give ourselves.

Your Picture of the "Ideal" Family

What are some ways that we get in our own way when we try to live in biblical wisdom with our families? In my experience, it often starts with trying to fit our family into a preconceived mold. Perhaps you have a picture of the "ideal" family in your mind right now. (Most of us do.) Maybe the children are always respectful, the parents are always calm, and family devotions are deep and engaging. When you compare your family to that ideal, it's easy to feel defeated. Or perhaps your ideal family is more about accomplishments. The children get all "As," they excel at sports, and have lots of friends. We are all good at finding fami-lies that seem to have it way more together than we do.

But consider this: Is it possible that your picture of the ideal family is keeping you from understanding and loving your *actual* family in the ways God has in mind? Does your image of the ideal family help or hinder you to live out the two great com-mandments to love God and others (Matthew 22:37–40)?

When we start by wanting our families to fit a preconceived mold, it's a small step to begin looking for a parenting formula that will help us achieve that ideal. What are some of the parent-ing formulas you have encountered? As a counselor, I have inter-acted with many parents who were trying to make a child-rearing formula work for their family. There always seems to be a new recipe for parenting success that guarantees that, if you follow it correctly, the result will be well-behaved, God-fearing young men and women.

Beyond Parenting Formulas

For example, years ago, there was a popular theory that parents should force their very young children into rigid schedules of eating and napping. The promised result was well-rounded, well-behaved children. But the best it could offer was highly structured homes. It was simply assumed that this structure was universally beneficial and the only correct way to parent.

As a result, many families tried to force their children into a formula that wasn't helpful for them. The idea wasn't completely bad; it was, in fact, beneficial to some families. The problem was that it was held up as "the only right way" to parent. A principle that worked well for some families became the model for all Christian parenting, and all were held to that standard.

Many parents felt like failures when this structure did not work for their family. Others felt frustrated because it forced them to parent outside their natural strengths and gifting, or it forced children who were wired differently into a mold that did not fit them. It did not make them calmer and better behaved; rather, it kept them from thriving according the way they were individually created.

That's what happens when we take something that is not an "essential" and make it a moral parenting imperative. Let's say that you are a parent who comes to life after 9:00 p.m. You work more effectively at that hour. You accomplish more around the house, and you and your spouse have more meaningful conversations with your children, who are also wired to enjoy late nights. Family life comes alive in the evening, and the house does not wake up till late morning (at least on weekends!). Contrast that with a family full of morning people, who cheerfully rise at the crack of dawn and go to bed by eight o'clock. Is one family more spiritually mature and godly because of their schedule? Or can we simply agree that they are just different? The truth is, wisdom and maturity are revealed in the way parents live their lives before the Lord and with their families—not in what time everyone goes to bed.

What about other parenting models that purport to depict the "ideal" family: the two-parent home where Dad works, Mom stays home to do the cooking and cleaning, and their two to three children all are smart, healthy, and struggle-free? Some families may conform to that ideal, but it is not the norm set forth in Scripture. In the Bible and in life, families are filled with individuals with differing gifts, aptitudes, hobbies, and skills. They are best guided by biblical wisdom, not the latest formula. Biblical wisdom equips you to create a home that is attentive to the individual people God has placed within it, so that you can raise your children to follow the Lord, and you can all live together in a Christ-centered way.

Sometimes these models seem very appealing; that is, until we realize that our families cannot live up to them. For example, perhaps I have a certain preference or ideal when it comes to educating my children. But what if I have a child who cannot fit into that model? Maybe the child has a disability—or exceptional intellectual gifts—and this requires me to think outside the box when it comes to his education. Should I keep trying to force my child to fit into my old ideal or should I forego my old preference for the sake of my child? By shaping my choice according to the gifts and needs of my child, I am doing what is truly ideal and loving him well.

Clinging to a certain model of family life or the "ideal" Christian home can get in the way of truly loving the family you have been given. Consider how such models and formulas might impact people whose life circumstances make it impossible for them to conform to a particular ideal. What do you tell the widow or single parent who must fill the roles of both mom and dad? What do you do when life presents you with a less-than-ideal family structure? Does that mean that a godly home life is not possible for you?

Consider parents who have physical or emotional limitations that prevent them from fulfilling a particular role in the home. Perhaps what they are capable of falls outside the norm we usually envision. What about a family where the father stays home or works part-time while the mother has a full-time career? What about the child with significant medical needs who requires a great deal of time and attention? How does a family structure home life to accommodate this? Consider the single adults who feel called to adopt or foster children: Are they outside God's best? Will their ability to form a biblical, loving environment always be inferior? As these examples demonstrate, you cannot come up with a simple, standard formula to fit every situation. One size cannot fit all, nor should it. Whether you are in a single parent or two-parent home, a commitment to follow the Lord and biblical wisdom is what should guide you.

These scenarios force us to evaluate our biases about what we believe makes an ideal family. Do I assume that a certain family structure or family size makes for a good home? Do I think a particular procedure, disciplinary method, or daily routine will automatically produce a good family?

The answer we need as parents is not a formula for our families. I believe we should be looking at something far more challenging. Instead of providing a parenting recipe, God calls parents to think biblically, wisely, and carefully about what love looks like in their unique family. This calling requires an absolute dependence on godly wisdom, on spiritual discernment regarding my family, and on personal holiness to be what my family needs me to be. The goal is a home centered on Christ.

This is not a formula I submit myself to, but neither is it a license to do whatever seems right in my own eyes. Far from it! Rather, it means a commitment to understanding Scripture's principles of godly relationships and the call and responsibility to lead a home.

God the Father as Our Model

> See what kind of love the Father has given to us, that
> we should be called children of God; and so we are.
> (1 John 3:1)

How do we know how to raise and love our children well?
We look to the One who is *our* Father. What has God done for
us? How does he demonstrate his love toward us? How does he
handle our sins and our sufferings, our struggles and fears, our
gifting and circumstances?

God describes himself as a father and us as his children. He
models how we are to live in relationships in our families. God
our Father is compassionate, gracious, steadfast in love, and slow
to anger. This is how he describes himself from Exodus 34:6–7:

> The LORD passed before him and proclaimed, "The
> LORD, the LORD, a God merciful and gracious, slow to
> anger, and abounding in steadfast love and faithfulness,
> keeping steadfast love for thousands, forgiving iniquity
> and transgression and sin, but who will by no means
> clear the guilty, visiting the iniquity of the fathers on the
> children and on the children's children to the third and
> fourth generation."

God as father is faithful to his children. He is steadfast in
his love toward us. His love for his children is long-suffering
and persevering, an unfaltering commitment to our good despite
circumstances.

Even in the midst of great grief and tragedy brought on by
Israel's bad behavior, God demonstrates how he lives out his love
to his people. In Lamentations 3:22, the author declares God's
character: "The steadfast love of the LORD never ceases; his mercies never come to an end; they are new every morning; great is
your faithfulness."

Verses 32 and 33 go on to say, "Though he cause grief, he will have compassion according to the abundance of his steadfast love; for he does not afflict from his heart or grieve the children of men."

Despite the suffering he endured, Job's words testify to God's specific, fatherly care: "You have granted me life and steadfast love, and your care has preserved my spirit" (Job 10:12). We can believe that in the midst of our hardest moments, God is intimately aware and present. No matter the circumstances or the sufferings that befall us, God can be trusted. He is for us, looking out for our interests and directing our steps. Our confidence is in his character: he is a loving Father.

Envision your children having that kind of confidence in you and your steadfast love toward them; in your utter commitment to their good. What a wonderful goal—to grow as parents who love our children the way our heavenly Father loves us! Instead of a formula, that is a calling—our calling.

God's Personal Love

Our heavenly Father's love is not only faithful, kind, persevering, and steadfast, it is also personal. He does not treat us all the same. He meets us individually, he understands our hearts and motives, and he convicts, encourages, and shepherds us according to our needs.

Several years ago, our family experienced a house fire. It destroyed our home, everything we owned, and took the lives of all our pets. We each experienced the grief and loss in different ways. I noticed that one child became withdrawn. Another was outwardly angry; another wanted to talk about it all the time. I was deeply impacted in a multitude of ways while also trying to shepherd our children through the loss. We were cared for and blessed immensely by our church, work, friends, and community. In numerous ways, these things were evidence of God's care and kindness toward us through others. Then there were more personal moments when God met us; times when I was alone, hurting, and questioning, and God would bring verses to mind, songs on the radio, people who would call, write notes, and say just what only the Lord knew I needed to hear. What ministered to my husband, Greg, was different but equally meaningful.

As parents we needed to address each of our kids' suffering individually. One needed to be drawn out, cry, and know it was okay, that God cared about her suffering. Another talked about his fears and concerns that it might happen again. Another needed help to process his anger at God for allowing the fire to happen. There was no one-size-helps-all approach. God's Word, his character, and his truth did not change, but how we contextualized them to each person's suffering did. We were given the task of discerning where each child was struggling so that we could speak truth, comfort, and hope. We needed to model Christ's love and care to them in the midst of their personal grief.

We see God's individual care for his people throughout the Bible. He cares for Abraham and Sarah by providing them with a son in their old age, and by speaking into their individual doubt or confusion. He provides just the right bride for Isaac. Jacob, despite his lies and deceit, is still under God's specific care as God gives him a vision of heaven and wrestles him to the ground. In 1 Kings 19, God models this in the way he comes to Elijah. Elijah is running for his life. He is fearful and tired. God provides food and water for him, and then addresses him personally. He knows what Elijah needs and meets him there. God spoke into David's sin very powerfully and personally through a story and the prophet Nathan. God knew to send particular prophets to particular nations and cities to deliver personalized messages they needed to hear. We could go on and on!

Christ Models God's Personal Love

Jesus is a living example of God's steadfast love toward us. God the Father sent his only Son to live among us and die for us. He is the ultimate expression of God's fatherly care. In Jesus, we see God's commitment to rescue us at great personal sacrifice. No greater love exists.

In Jesus's life on earth, he modeled specific care and personal interaction to those he encountered. The woman at the well was known intimately and given grace despite her many sins. Zacchaeus, a tax collector, was sought out for fellowship. The Pharisees and Sadducees were rebuked and called a brood of vipers. Each disciple was known individually. Jesus often demonstrated that he knew them so well that he knew what they were thinking! And then he spoke into their doubt, unbelief, fear, and devotion.

When Jesus lived on earth, he was a living picture of the love of God in action. We know that kindness and forgiveness are relational biblical principles for our family life. Why? Because we are called to forgive as Christ has forgiven us. Jesus forgave those who mistreated him. We are called to do the same. Jesus was kind. We are called to kindness. Paul sums up our call to be kind and forgiving toward one another like this: "Be kind to one another, tenderhearted, forgiving one another, as God in Christ forgave you" (Ephesians 4:32).

Has Christ forgiven me in the same ways I must forgive others? In principle, yes. In application, the ways I need to forgive my children and the ways they must forgive me often vary. They may need forgiveness for disobedience or dishonesty; I may need it for frustration or a short temper. But our need for humility and forgiveness is the same. We often tell our kids, "All ground is level at the cross. We need Jesus just as much as you do." Our struggles may look different, but our need is always the same. We are all wandering sheep, in need of a Shepherd to lead us, guide us, and bring us back when we are prone to wander away.

Wisdom Found in Christ

In 1 Corinthians 1:30–31 it states, "And because of him, you are in Christ Jesus, who became to us wisdom from God, righteousness and sanctification and redemption, so that, as it is written, 'Let the one who boasts, boast in the Lord.'"

Wisdom is incarnated in a person, Christ. He is God's wisdom to us, and he lives out God's wisdom perfectly for us. He is the image of God and demonstrates to us how to be an image bearer. God's wisdom is not found in worldly knowledge or methodologies, the latest research, or seemingly brilliant parenting formulas. Christ is the model of God's character for us, living out the life we are called to live. He images the Father, and he calls us to follow him and be made like him.

When we seek to live independently from God, we become foolish. Adam and Eve sought to know wisdom apart from what God had given them. They heard from God himself, yet they were enticed and corrupted by what they wanted to hear. We look to establish homes based on worldly wisdom or what we believe is best. In our big goals (well-educated children, successful lives) or small ones (peace for an evening or children who will do their homework), we are often unwise in what we seek in our parenting. We are always called to reorient our homes away from what seems wise from a worldly perspective toward homes dependent on God's guidance. Biblical wisdom comes from living under God's truth and revelation, Christ's model to us, and the Spirit's guidance and help.

This means that my ultimate goal is not even the good desires I have for our family, things like peace and quiet and obedient, moral children. My ultimate desire is to be a parent whose life rests on what has been graciously been given to me by the Father, modeled to me in Christ Jesus, and supplied to me by his Spirit.

The Waterfall Effect

The more we base our family relationships on the way God relates to us and cares for us, the more we can stop relying on formulas to direct us. Instead of parenting "how-tos" and formulas, we rely on who God is in relationship to us. We ask him for wisdom on how to reflect his love in our family. I can comfort my children in their struggles because of the comfort I have been given (2 Corinthians 1:4). I can forgive and bear with my children, just as Christ has forgiven me (Colossians 3:13). I discipline my children because my Creator lovingly, caringly disciplines me (Proverbs 3:12). I choose to love sacrificially because it was first done for me and I choose to be a fragrant offering in my home (Ephesians 5:2).

God lavishes his love on us and it flows through us to others. That's the waterfall effect. We love, forgive, give grace, instruct, encourage, admonish, and discipline according to the need of the moment with the grace that God supplies. Our heavenly Father does not respond to us with a cookie-cutter approach. He knows us personally, and he speaks intimately and specifically to us, according to our need.

As we learn more about God's love for us and live in his love, the waterfall of that love flows through us into our relationships. Philippians 2:3–4 says, "Do nothing from selfish ambition or conceit, but in humility count others more significant than yourselves. Let each of you look not only to his own interests, but also to the interests of others." All that we do is shaped by a commitment to mutual edification, sacrifice, building up one another, and offering grace in the midst of weakness. Every parenting choice we make is marked by the character qualities of a personal God who demonstrates intimate knowledge of us and extends patience, lovingkindness, and guidance to us.

The family is a body, a community where there is authority and leadership, but also a reciprocal nature of ministry and need. Parents are in a position of decision-making and authority, but also respect each person's individuality and uniqueness. All work together for the good of the whole. All are equally valuable and necessary, and all learn to engage life together.

Parents and children need Christ equally and are able to express Christlikeness equally. All can confess sin and offer forgiveness. All need grace and can extend it. Each one is at a different level of spiritual maturity, but all can demonstrate a commitment to follow Jesus. All pursue mutual edification in humility, having the posture that they are "for each other," not against each other. When one person is struggling, everyone should be there to help, encourage, pray, and remind each other of what is true and good.

This is not an easy or natural way to relate to one another in families. I speak with many families in which the working attitude is "every man for himself." If one person fails, everyone abandons ship, runs for the hills, points and says, "I told you so," or criticizes. Imagine living in a very different community, where no one wants to see you fail. They aren't waiting to expose your failure to prove that they are superior to you. Rather, they lift you up when you are weak; they are forgiving and gracious when you have sinned against them. They know your worst and your best, and they love you regardless. That is living out the spirit of Ephesians to "be kind to one another, tenderhearted, forgiving one another, as God in Christ forgave you" (Ephesians 4:32).

We often remind our kids that we all struggle with sin. We all need to meet Christ at the foot of the cross; parents and children alike need forgiveness and daily grace. As parents, we fail, have our flaws, love imperfectly, and need grace. Not only do we all need Christ, but we also are all living together in a community, to mutually sharpen one another and help one another toward godliness.

Paul and the New Testament Churches: A Model for Family Life

We don't have to look any further than the New Testament to see biblical principles of life together applied specifically. When we read Paul's letters to the early churches, we observe him addressing each church individually, according to its specific needs. He offers personalized correction, rebuke, encouragement, reminders, cautions, praise, and hope to each church. What Paul says to the church in Ephesus is different from what he says to the church in Philippi. Why? Because they wrestled with different issues. Biblical truths, worship, and practices had taken on various forms and customs. Creative liberty was given to some, while others needed rebuke for losing sight of the truth.

Each church faced specific challenges. They needed wisdom to respond to heretics, to specific sins in their community, and to a wrong view of the law. They had to deal with challenging individuals and circumstances. Particular gifts and persons who excelled in service were commended by Paul as examples to others. Every church body was distinct; a God-given individuality was always assumed. The way a church lived out that individuality was sometimes celebrated and sometimes corrected.

Like families, church bodies can get distracted by trying to create formulas for the "correct" way to "do church," rather than granting each other freedom to be godly according to the needs of their body. We all have something to learn from the strengths, weaknesses, gifts, or mission of another church. However, we must not turn this into a fixed, mechanical approach for living the Christian life.

Instead (once again like families), churches need to be committed to the principles of Christian living that are universal, and truth that is unwavering, not open to debate or personal preference. Paul consistently called New Testament churches back to foundational biblical truth. We have the same call to imitate Christlikeness in our personal lives and in community with others. But there is liberty in our expression of biblical truths and principles.

One example is foot washing. Foot washing was modeled by Jesus with his disciples. It was an example of humility and service, qualities we are all entreated to emulate. Yet not every church practiced foot washing, and very few churches do today. Why? Because it was a practice that was culturally informed. The principles of humility and service are universal and unchanging, but the way they are practiced may be shaped by the needs of the church body you are in. Foot washing might be seen as archaic and unnecessary, while cleaning a neighbor's garage or bathing a quadriplegic demonstrates the same quality of humility.

There are many parallels to family life. We must be committed to the unchanging truths of God's Word while also granting freedom to live them out in a way that edifies the family God has given you. This requires a dependence on God that fuels a dedication to personal holiness and a tenacious commitment to wisdom. Wisdom requires discernment; it necessitates letting go of formulas and instead asking God for insight to see the needs within your family and to respond thoughtfully and unselfishly.

Often we try to establish a structured regime, following a formula for having good kids, a happy home, or a "model family." Might we be serving the wrong agenda? We are allowing the judgments or critiques of others to shape the way we establish our homes. Do you allow outside sources to pressure you into a parenting role that does not fit who God made you to be? Instead, we should celebrate the uniqueness God has placed in each individual and family, and live out his love and wisdom in the midst of that uniqueness.

The Metaphor of the Body

Romans 12:4–6a reads, "For as in one body we have many members, and the members do not all have the same function, so we, though many, are one body in Christ, and individually members of one another. Having gifts that differ according to the grace given to us, let us use them. . . ."

First Corinthians 12:14–27 also uses the body as a metaphor for the church of Christ. Here we see the principle that not all members function in similar ways or with equal authority, but all are of value. No parts are less a part of the body; all deserve to have honor bestowed on them. I believe that we are to consider each member of a family in a similar way. Each one is an integral part of the community. They are not all given the same gifts, the same role, or the same perceived level of honor, authority, or prominence, but each is there to work within the whole. Each one is there to be a blessing and to be blessed in the family.

In the body of Christ, it sometimes appears that we value conformity and uniformity over individuality. Our God is a creative God who has demonstrated his creativity, personality, and uniqueness in every aspect of nature. I believe that God intends to give that same kind of liberty to families in the way they live out their lives. Clearly, Scripture's principles for relationship are the foundation and guardrails for the way we express our individual uniqueness. Within that framework, families can live in a way that's glorifying to God, loving to one another, and truly unique according to their needs and their gifts.

The End Result

Most of the time, parents are working to see changes in behavior: children who no longer lie or fight with their siblings, who complete homework or chores, or who demonstrate obedience and compliance. Unfortunately, this is often pursued in ways that fail to model grace and steadfast love. Building bridges with our children takes time and effort. We need to consistently spend the time and energy necessary to demonstrate the character of Christ to our children so that they can see that we truly do have their best interests at heart.

Can you see the difference? One approach values a child's compliance and good behavior; the other wants God's character to be shared by the parent with the child. These two approaches need not be mutually exclusive but, sadly, they often are. God calls us to be what we need to be as parents even if our children do not respond as we hope. This frees us to love them and respond wisely to them, and to have hope even when we do not yet see the fruit of our labor.

Why is this so? If our desire to model Jesus's character to our children is greater than our desire to have them act a certain way, this allows us to respond to them in ways that are consistent with Christ's character instead of ways that reflect our frustrated lesser desires, like anger and attempts to control them. We are guided by the Spirit instead of our fleshly desires. Having done this, we can rest in the fact we have done the most important piece of parenting. Whether our children then change or not depends on their hearts' interaction with God's Spirit and his Word.

More than Behavior Change

Most of us tend to worry about the behaviors we are aware of in our kids' lives: vaping, porn, masturbation, lack of motivation in school, self-injury, peer obsession, anxiety, or disobedience. As we've seen, parenting formulas focus mainly on changing behavior, and we do, of course, want good kids, happy, peaceful homes, and godly families. But how quickly those good things can become idolatrous demands! These good but out-of-control desires drive us to poor parenting to achieve the desired outcome.

But when we are motivated by a love for God and our children, our parenting choices are no longer driven by our need to attain particular results. My parenting is no longer controlled by my personal motives, agenda, fears, or hopes, even when those desired outcomes are good things. When we focus on what *our* role should be in our children's lives and on knowing them personally, we focus less on their behavioral improvements and more on how the Lord is calling us to shepherd them.

Focusing on our role will also require us to evaluate own responses in family life. We will always wrestle with our own sins in parenting, and we must always be mindful of how our agenda can subtly warp our parenting choices. Do not be afraid to be humble before your children, to apologize for your sins and seek their forgiveness. It shows them that we all need the Savior. It endears you to your children when you walk alongside them, not as a perfect person, but as someone who can sympathize with their weaknesses.

When our focus as parents shifts to reflecting the image of Christ, we no longer see our children as personal achievements that bring us glory or shame. We begin to see them as fellow strugglers with whom we live, eat, grieve, forgive, and do life. They are people who are entrusted to our care; individuals we strive to know well, speak to meaningfully, and love unwaveringly. As 3 John 1:4 reminds us, we should have no greater joy than that our children walk in truth.

It's Never Too Late

Perhaps as you read this, you are filled with regret (a universal parental pastime, I'm afraid). You feel as if you've already blown it with your kids, or you've instilled fear and unrealistic standards in your home. Perhaps you have been driven by your need for your children to love you and affirm you as a parent. Maybe you've been driven to insist on outward compliance and good, moral character. Maybe you've held yourself or your children to unhelpful standards. Still, you can turn things around.

Whether your children are toddlers, teenagers, or adults, it is never too late. There is always an opportunity to repent and restore. Relationships can change and healing can occur. Regardless of how long you've been parenting and how old your children are, it is never too late to turn the ship around. There may be more work to do (or undo), there may be failures to confess, and there may be relationships to be restored. But the Spirit can intercede and bring life to the lifeless places in your home. As parents, we must never give up building bridges with our kids.

Parenting is rewarding but exhausting. It overflows with to-do lists, schedules to manage, problems to solve, and trips to kids' appointments, sports, clubs, and youth group. I've heard many parents say that they woke up one day and wondered where the time had gone, because they feel so disconnected from their children. We easily get caught up in demanding routines even though we wish things were different.

Don't let this be your story. It is never too early to start doing things differently, and it is never too late. Do what is countercultural, because even passively submitting to society's norms for parenting can turn into a formula that rules your home. I hope this book challenges you to question such things and their impact on your family. I hope it frees you to begin brainstorming about how your family might live in meaningful, rich ways.

We all are tempted to look for the perfect family and attempt to replicate it. We hope that if we just punch in the right formula, our children will turn out just right. Unfortunately, many parents feel defeated because they've tried the formula, and it didn't produce what they expected. I say, be thankful it did not work, because it was never intended for you.

Instead, envision a family where there are imperfect people, many trials, and unwavering love. Imagine a home where brokenness and hope, temptations and forgiveness coexist. Where failures meet mercies that are new every morning. Where all members are in equal need and receive an equal measure of grace.

Be encouraged. This is what we have all been given. Regardless of where you find yourself right now, take heart. Change can happen.

Parenting Tool Box
How to Conduct a Family Evaluation

Sit down by yourself or with your spouse and examine the family God has given you. Who is part of your home? What are the contributions, roles, strengths, weaknesses, struggles, giftings, and needs of each member? Write your answers down and include the thoughts and input of each person whenever possible.

Now, consider your parenting. How does knowing these things begin to shape the way you should parent the children God has given you? Where does God speak very directly into the particulars of each person? Where are the places that feel tough to figure out, requiring extra wisdom, prayer, and perhaps outside input?

Be aware that as your family grows, ages, and matures, your parenting, your rules, your roles, and the way you set up your home will adapt as well.

Brainstorm about how this might shape how you establish your home life. How does this inform family rules, parenting, and schedules? What do healthy levels of freedom, responsibility, and privilege look like for each family member?

Reflection Questions

1. Do you tend to talk more about the disciplines or the delights of living with your children?
2. What parenting formulas are you tempted to try?
3. How can you move toward wisdom and away from formula? What might that look like for you?
4. Why might the idea of freedom feel scary to a parent?
5. Name some of your fears about your children's behavior.
6. What are your spoken or unspoken expectations for your home and family?

CHAPTER 2

Christ-Centered Parenting

Most parents who are picking up this book already love their children. We want to be better parents. Much of our struggle is not about *whether* we care for our family, but *how* we care for our family. The last chapter discussed living out of biblical principles instead of parenting formulas. I hope that resonated with you, but it also might have left you with even more questions. If not a formula, then what?

Child-rearing is hard work. Fighting against cultural norms at times feels unachievable. Defying time constraints and hectic schedules to mentor and educate our children seems like an uphill battle. Letting go of parenting formulas might seem like just one more burden to add—now we have to figure it all out for ourselves!

But the alternative to a formula is not depending on your own strength and wisdom. It's going to God and asking him for the daily help you need to live out of his love for your children. It means asking him to help you nurture your family. What does that mean? Simply to cultivate God's character and express his love in your family life. This can only be done when we are emptied of our own sense of competency and realize that the task requires far more than we have within us.

The Waterfall Effect

We talked in the last chapter about "the waterfall effect," where every good and perfect gift flows from above. Any ability we have to nurture our families flows down from Father, the source of all that is good and worthy of imitating.

To be a good parent requires us to sacrifice many of our own desires to provide for the needs of our children. When we do this, we model a selfless Christlikeness that lives out the truths of Scripture and invites young people to know Christ personally.

We have been given the Spirit of Christ to help us to cultivate all that is virtuous and pure in relationships. We love because he first loved us; we forgive as we have been forgiven; we live sacrificially because he gave himself up for us. When we commit to nurturing family relationships, we want our actions, words, and character to flow from what we have received from Christ.

We often hear that imitation is the sincerest form of flattery. Several years ago, I came home from a long, tiring day. My two daughters, then ages three and four, were full of energy. I sat down on the floor with them and instinctively they began playing with my hair. Within seconds, they were pulling out all the girly barrettes, hair clips, and glittery hair accessories they could find.

Feeling relieved that they were occupied and I could relax, I closed my eyes, and endured the yanking, pulling, and creative mess they were making of my hair. I was slowly being transformed into a Medusa-type creature with snake-like appendages coming out from all directions. At one point Brittney, the four-year-old, ran into the bathroom and put the brush under the water in the sink to get it wet. Every morning the girls had watched me take a hairbrush and run it under the water in order to smooth out their hair and untangle the knots. Brittney was having a ball, and continued to run in and out of the bathroom wetting the hairbrush and then wetting my hair. Her little sister, Kimmy, picked up on the idea and began doing the same. About the third or fourth time they ran into the bathroom, it dawned on me that Kimmy couldn't reach the sink. How was she getting the hairbrush wet? That was enough to get me off the floor and, sure enough, as I crawled over to the bathroom door and looked in, there was Kimmy dipping the hairbrush into the toilet. (Later in the evening I also found anti-bacterial soap in my hair, so I could only hope that the two cancelled each other out.)

Although creative, Kimmy's imitation of me was grossly off. I would like to think she got the spirit of it but missed the details (important details if you ask the one affected by it). In a similar vein, I often wonder how far off I am in my imitation of Christ. How often do I take principles and passages and attempt to implement them based on my own limitations and distorted understanding?

I wonder how true this is of us all when we hear the call to imitate Christ in our family relationships. I'd like to think that I love my family the way Christ calls me to: that I refrain from anger and malice, and that I am forgiving. But in my honest moments, I know I rely far too much on my own virtue and strength to accomplish this. I am sure my self-reliance translates very poorly. I need to draw on something—on Someone— outside myself. On my own, I lack the resources to be what is asked.

Nurturing Relationships

Philippians 2:3–5 says, "Do nothing from selfish ambition or conceit, but in humility count others more significant than yourselves. Let each of you look not only to his own interests, but also to the interests of others. Have this mind among yourselves, which is yours in Christ Jesus. . . ."

When I read this passage, I immediately start to think about how I can do this—how *I* might muster up the moral fortitude to be these things to my family. I look for ways to be a kinder, more compassionate spouse and parent. I strive to be a role model in my home and with extended family, to demonstrate compassion and care for others. Being and acting like Jesus Christ honestly requires far more than I have within myself, yet my first reaction is often to look for some type of formula for humility or godliness.

What God has asked of you and me can never be accomplished by sheer human grit and determination. Hear that again: what Christ calls you to can NEVER be accomplished by sheer human determination.

This cuts to the heart of why we often fail to nurture meaningful relationships with our children. Time after time, the way I approach my family relationships is tainted with a subtle (or not so subtle) expectation of return. My responses can look godly, but I so easily inject an expectation that I will profit from my efforts; my children will in turn be gracious or kind to me.

Far too often, relationships fail and bitterness creeps in because the motivation behind our behavior is not a genuine giving of self or dying to self. Rather, we act with an expectation of a good return. We can forgive, be compassionate, and love our children, but with the expectation—and hidden desire, even demand—that we will reap a benefit. *That is the problem:* We give to get. We "self-sacrifice" to get something back. We love with the expectation of return.

The call to "do nothing out of selfish ambition" reveals our hearts. It exposes our expectations but, with that, it has the potential to set us free from ourselves. We may fear that letting go of "my right" to react might mean being taken advantage of. But as we live in grace with others, the truth is that we are not at the mercy of another human being. We are becoming what God created us to be—we have the mindset of Christ and we are liberated from ourselves.

A Human-Controlled Heart
vs. the Spirit-Transformed Heart

Much of what we do in our daily Christian living flows from a self-generated sense of morality. We attempt to express personal holiness through the strength of our character or a natural desire to be good. We are trying our best! But it's in relationships that we clearly see that self-generated goodness will not carry us far. The reality is that we are incapable of any uncorrupted good apart from Christ's life within us. Even nurturing relationships can become tainted by an idolatrous need to find personal validation from what our family gives us. I cannot possibly love my needy children sacrificially unless I have the mind of Christ. My own mind gives to get. But Paul reminds us that the solution to our most basic relationship problems is the mind of Christ. This is a new mind that acts as a waterfall, with the love of Christ flowing down on us, filling us with God's love, making us more like Christ, and pouring out of us to others. This is what nurturing relationships are meant to be.

Anyone who has lived in a family knows that in the toughest moments of relational conflicts, our personal moral reserve will not stand against the difficulty of the moment. Moments when I discover that my daughter has been deceiving us and sneaking out at night, or when my son is caught with drugs in school. When I am called to "suffer for others" while feeling personally sinned against, misunderstood, or underappreciated, I am powerless against bitterness and an unforgiving spirit. Only a divinely renewed heart that clings to grace can overcome evil with good. Only Christ enables me to lay down my life and my rights for the benefit of another.

Consider Maggie and John, who found out that their son Tyler was texting a friend, saying that he was suicidal and hated his family. They were distraught to uncover what he really thought and to find out that he had been involved in dangerous behaviors that put the whole family in jeopardy. Up to that point, they thought they had a healthy, open relationship. They hung out together, laughed, joked, and talked about Tyler's day in school. John and Tyler even enjoyed attending a father-son Bible study together.

Despite overwhelming evidence and his own texts, Tyler denied everything adamantly. He refused to talk about what his parents had uncovered, accused them of not trusting him, and was angry that they were checking up on him. John and Maggie were reeling; they felt betrayed and confused. Everything within them wanted to yell, accuse him, and respond with severe consequences. They were faced with the difficult task of renouncing their own right to be angry and asking the Lord how to minister to their wayward son. In such difficult parenting moments, only a Spirit-driven response can look beyond the pain your child is causing and instead reply to the need of the moment.

John and Maggie wrestled through their own emotions and acknowledged their desire to force Tyler to open up so that they could fix whatever was going on inside him. They floundered, but they were committed to loving Tyler and trying to draw him out. When they were tempted to be discouraged or frustrated, they reminded themselves that this needed to be a work of the Spirit, and they needed to concentrate on what God was calling them to do.

It took time and many moments of denial, rejection, and dead ends, but Tyler slowly began to share his loneliness, his struggle with perfectionism, and his fear of disappointing them. They pursued counseling for Tyler, and he later shared that it was his parents' persevering kindness and persistence that impacted him most. He'd noticed that they no longer were preoccupied with changing his behavior, but were resolute to personally understand him and how they could love him.

Nurturing Conversations

> Let no corrupting talk come out of your mouths, but only such as is good for building up, as fits the occasion, according to their needs, that it may give grace to those who hear. And do not grieve the Holy Spirit of God, by whom you were sealed for the day of redemption. Let all bitterness and wrath and anger and clamor and slander be put away from you, along with all malice. Be kind

to one another, tenderhearted, forgiving one another, as God in Christ forgave you. (Ephesians 4:29–32)

Conversations are risky, aren't they? Recently I was driving down a road with all six of my kids in the car. I often say that our best conversations happen in the car; everyone is strapped in with nowhere to go. We happened to drive by an adult bookstore and one of my kids asked, "What is an adult bookstore, Mom?" Those are the times I am tempted to change the subject, ask them if they'd like to go for pizza, and wonder why my husband never is in the car when I need him.

I decided to answer by explaining broadly what it was and why it wasn't a place any grown-up should go into—an honest, tactful response without going into too much detail (or so I thought). One of my kids said that adult bookstores were mentioned in a book he was reading, which gave me insight into what my kids were exposed to and allowed me to engage well on a tough topic.

Fast-forward a week or so and we are driving to someone's home for dinner. As we are driving down the street, our six-year-old says to my husband, "Look, it is the *parent* bookstore." What?! No, that is definitely not a parent store. I could only imagine him walking into Sunday school one morning and saying, "Mommy and Daddy have a bookstore . . ." One more example of how things can get lost in translation.

Still, hard or uncomfortable conversations are worth the risk of misunderstanding because we want to proactively shape our children's understanding.

In our home, we have two questions based on this passage in Ephesians 4: Are you building up or tearing down? And do your words or actions give life or decay?

We are given two inventories here. One is of destructive behaviors and speech; the other is of self-giving grace. We see how we are called to be transformed from the futility of our thinking to represent Christ and his grace through our interactions with others.

We are challenged to pursue nurturing conversations for the purpose of building others up and giving grace. We are called to imitate Christ by giving grace to our family, speaking truth in order to build up, not tear down. I don't speak truth to my child so that I will benefit from the exchange. Rather, I speak to pour forth grace so that Christ will look all the more glorious to them. I am to give what I have received.

In verse 29 we read, "Let no corrupting talk [anything unconstructive, inedible, lacking value] come out of your mouths, but only such as is good for building up [that which is constructive] as fits the occasion, that it may give grace [benefit] to those who hear."

Here is a place where the translation don't quite do the verse justice. Language is so important! The intent here is to speak in a way that is constructive, fit for consumption, and edible versus that which is indigestible or rotten. Our words are called to give grace and life to our listeners.

Years ago there was a documentary called *Super Size Me*. If you saw it, you'll remember that it is enough to keep you away from fast food for quite a while. In the film, a man looks at the effects of fast food on the human body, using himself as the guinea pig. For one month, he eats nothing but McDonald's, ordering everything on the menu and "super-sizing" his order whenever asked. The result is a sobering examination of how people feed themselves and the role the food industry plays in it.

In less than thirty days, the man goes from being a healthy, energetic man with normal blood counts and good cholesterol to an unhealthy man who is regularly nauseous, weak, and lethargic. He is being affected physically by the food he is consuming and all the doctors monitoring him urge him to stop his experiment.

This man found out that *sustenance does not equal nourishment*. Simply putting food into your body does not mean that it's good for you or contains any nutritional value.

That is also true of our words. How many families coexist for long periods of time living on "fast food" interaction? It keeps things going, it communicates the necessities, but it lacks any nutritional value. It lacks meaningful intimacy, any true revealing of oneself or any effort to really know another. How often do we sit with our children and truly seek to know and be known? How often do we see this happen at holiday dinners or family reunions? I will go a step further to say that not only is our speech often lacking anything that edifies and gives grace, it often becomes the very thing that erodes the relationship.

Our speech is not neutral. It will either give grace to others or it will lead to decay. Does it offer grace to the person before me or does it delight in finding fault? Is it constructive or does it leave a bad taste in the mouth?

Christ poured out himself for us in our need. We are to imitate him through our relationships, not for our personal profit, but for the benefit of anyone in need. The words I speak to others will either make Christ real to them or irrelevant. They will provide value and nourishment or they will become decay.

This call does not hinder me from speaking into my most intimate relationships, but it defines the way I do it. If my daughter is speaking to her family with contempt and hostility, I do not come down on her with all my parental authority, shaming her into an apology. I try to address her sin out of concern for her well-being. I speak so that she hears consideration and a regard for who she is, not condemnation. I am not prevented from addressing poor behavior, but my words are shaped by considering the person's best interests.

Nurturing through Forgiveness

Notice the waterfall effect with our call to forgive: "forgiving one another, as God in Christ forgave you" (v. 32).

The following quote is attributed to Mark Twain, who is not otherwise known for his godly wisdom: "Forgiveness is the fragrance the violet sheds on the heel that has crushed it." What a descriptive picture of what Paul is talking about! When I am crushed by another's sin, what comes out of me will either be the pleasing aroma of Christ or a stench that reflects my self-centered desires. We cannot self-generate godly expressions of forgiveness, nor should we try. What comes out of us is what is already within us, which is why it is so important to allow Christ's life to live in us.

What about a self-centered, strong-willed child who takes every opportunity to promote his own agenda in a home? Family dinners are constantly fraught with arguments and disagreements; holidays are spoiled with selfish demands for more gifts or more fun. Every morning is a fight to get the child dressed, his homework or chores done, and out the door. A child like this wearies everyone in a home. It is tempting to allow yourself to become more quick-tempered, less tolerant and kind, and more tolerant of the negative reactions of others in the home because you share their frustrations. The difficulty of dealing with the identified "difficult person" can excuse all kinds of unloving, bitter reactions. In contrast, Paul's entreaty to live as a fragrant offering means that I am prepared to forgive and give grace. I choose to die to my own right to be weary and frustrated and choose instead to love. When this happens, I am not only loving sacrificially like Christ, but I am modeling that kind of love to all of my children. I am creating an environment that encourages Christlike one-anothering.

Forgiveness that expresses itself to my family as an offering and sacrifice becomes a sweet fragrance to the heel that has crushed me. It becomes the aroma of Christ that draws those around me to the power within me. It fosters a home filled with graciousness, a willingness to overlook an offense, and a persevering love that does not give up on another. It leaves an indelible impression on those who are watching—whether it is our children, our relatives, or fellow believers.

Nurturing through Sacrifice

> Therefore, be imitators of God, as beloved children. And walk in love, as Christ loved us and gave himself up for us, a fragrant offering and sacrifice to God. (Ephesians 5:1–2)

The image is that of the Old Testament sacrifices, where an offering was sacrificed on an altar and, as the fire consumed it, a pleasing aroma arose to God, a pleasing aroma that only comes with a sacrifice.

As a parent, you are called to give of yourself (an offering) and you are called to die to self (a sacrifice). There is no walking in love without some degree of giving and dying to ourselves. We can't emphasize grace for ourselves without also extending grace to others. We shouldn't be surprised when we struggle in families, when we fight off bitterness and resentment, when our words become a source of tension. When we respond with a willingness to bear the sufferings of others, others can see Christ in us.

As we sacrifice for others, we become a pleasing aroma to God and those we love. The call to sacrifice does not mean that we remain silent and passive. Jesus Christ did something very proactive and intentional when he laid his life down for us. Understanding this frees us to sacrifice in a way that is fragrant and pleasing, because my purpose for doing so is free from selfish motives. What pours forth then is the aroma of Christ in me and through me.

I have an uncle, Uncle Melly. He was born mentally incapacitated in an era when people like him were put away in institutions and kept from the public. There were no group homes, government services, or programs for the mentally handicapped. My grandparents' only choice was to raise him or to institutionalize him. They chose to keep him at home and raise him. This meant that my grandmother's life changed.

Uncle Melly's home was his world; therefore, it became her world. He was not able to go to school and there were no supports that came to the home. There was only my grandmother (and his six siblings as they got older) to care for him and engage him. My grandmother was a godly woman and an extraordinary example of a living offering and sacrifice. She cared for Uncle Melly twenty-four hours a day, without much reprieve. She taught her children to never be ashamed of him. She modeled a purposeful longsuffering that impacted her children as they grew in compassion and tenderness toward him.

As my uncle aged and my grandparents became more frail, my parents and several other siblings began to look for ways to take care of them all. One aunt and uncle in particular had remained single and they committed themselves to be the primary caretakers of my grandparents and uncle. My mom and others would offer to step in and give them occasional reprieves. Our family would invite Uncle Melly to our home for a weekend or a week, take him for rides in the car, buy him puzzles and teddy bears (all of which were given the name "Smokey"). As a child, I grew up around him and watched how my parents, aunt, and uncle cared for him. My siblings and I learned a great deal about compassion, acceptance, and not fearing those who were different. But perhaps what impacted me most was not the life of my uncle, but the example of my grandmother, parents, aunt, and uncle, who gave sacrificially of themselves over the years. There was often hardship and pain. Lives were impacted; personal agendas sacrificed. There was no personal return for them. They became givers rather than takers. They sought to provide what they had to give for the sake of another.

Their giving of themselves was not only a pleasing aroma then, it was the fragrance of Christ that drifted down to several generations after them. They left a legacy in our family that has impacted each of us in a multitude of ways. It's a legacy that, by God's grace, will be passed down to our children and our children's children.

The person transformed by Christ does not act out of a desire for personal gain. As this transformation takes place in my life, I no longer give to get. I learn to love my spouse, my children, and my most intimate relationships as a fragrant offering, holy and pleasing to God. Our families are most gratifying, our parenting most rewarding, our adult sibling relationships most fulfilling when the grace given to us spurs us to walk in love as Christ loved us. I give because I have received.

This all flows out of our identity as God's dearly loved children. We are deeply loved and connected; we are Christ's brothers and sisters, which gives us power outside ourselves. We are not only free to, but expected to, cling to a loving Father, who gives us what we do not naturally have within us. He supernaturally enables us to be what we were created to be. This is not a picture of servitude but of freedom. We have a picture of deep, meaningful relationship that liberates me from having to perform according to another's standard or formula. Rather, I am free to be who God created me to be in my relationships, my parenting, and my choices. This is not a picture of doing whatever feels good to me. It is a godliness expressed individually in my strengths, weaknesses, giftings, and calling. Family life becomes an expression of this as well.

In your homes and extended families, you want to celebrate the love and grace you've been given. You want to live with this kind of grace and you want to reflect it in your daily living. Nurturing a family is a lifestyle that makes Christ central. He is the source from which all that is good and holy flows.

Let me end with a vision for how to live out this grace we've been given. Here is what B. B. Warfield wrote in *Imitating the Incarnation*:

Self-sacrifice means not indifference to our times and our fellows: it means absorption in them. It means forgetfulness of self in others. It means entering into every man's hopes and fears, longings and despairs: it means manysideness of spirit, multiform activity, multiplicity of sympathies. It means richness of development. It means not that we should live one life, but a thousand lives— binding ourselves to a thousand souls by the filaments of so loving a sympathy that their lives become ours.

It means that all the experiences of men shall smite our souls and shall beat and batter these stubborn hearts of ours into fitness for their heavenly home. It is, after all, then, the path to the highest possible development, by which alone we can be made truly men.[1]

A Christ-centered home means that we are emptying our home of personal agendas, striving to image the Lord before our children. We are striving to love sacrificially, to engage with one another meaningfully, and to pour forth God's character in all we say and do. It does not mean perfection; it means humility in weakness. It means we give ourselves to him, and his strength is made perfect in our weakness. We become a channel of his life to others.

Parenting Tool Box
What Is Christ-Centered Parenting?

Christ-centered parenting means that we have not made our children the center of our home life so that all things revolve around them. Christ-centered parenting also means that we have not put parents on center stage so that all revolves around their desires, preferences, or needs. Rather, Christ is center stage. He is the reason all is said and done. A home is established with that in mind, as we seek to be like Christ in the way we care for our children.

How might this perspective change what you are currently doing as a parent? Does it convict you to change work schedules to

---

1. B. B. Warfield, "Imitating the Incarnation," from *The Savior of the World* (reprint: Carlisle, PA: Banner of Truth, 1990), 70.

be home more, stretch you to be more present in conversation, or spend more one-on-one time with a particular child? What would it look like for you to live sacrificially in your home? How does loving your family well require you to put aside personal agendas?

Most families can profit from meditating on specific passages of Scripture that are taped on the refrigerator, memorized weekly, or in other ways instilled in a child's day-to-day thinking. What might some of those passages be for your family? List the Scripture passages and parts of the gospel message that you feel need to come to life for your family.

What are some values that you want to instill in your children that are unique to your home and family? Might it be service, volunteering, giving, hospitality?

Reflection Questions

1. In what ways do you nurture relationships in your home? Are there things that get in the way?
2. What are some ways that you respond to your kids out of your own ability level?
3. What would change in your parenting if you knew that the Spirit of God was directing your responses?
4. Are there conversations you avoid in your home? Why?
5. What destructive patterns of communication do you see in your home? How would you like to see them change?
6. How can you nurture deeper, more meaningful conversations?
7. Would your children describe forgiveness as a character trait in your family? Why or why not? What are ways you could change this?
8. How has self-sacrifice been modeled to you? How might you strive to model it to your family?

CHAPTER 3

Becoming an Expert on Your Family

The purpose in a man's heart is like deep water, but a man of understanding will draw it out. (Proverbs 20:5)

Kelly came in to talk about some struggles with parenting her children. Kelly liked routines. She was often up at the crack of dawn and in bed by 8:00 p.m. She enjoyed staying on schedule, lived by the clock, and thrived on staying organized. Her daughter and son were a different story. Oliver, her husband, was a night owl and it seemed their son, Dylan, was too. It was a battle getting Dylan up in the morning and a battle getting him to bed at night. His best thinking happened after eight o'clock, when Kelly's brain was shutting down and she longed to have her children in bed and her day over. Her toddler daughter, Emily, had acute sensory issues, coupled with an asthma condition that made it difficult for her to sleep through the night. This meant that Emily often woke up throughout the night, and took shorter naps during the day. Because of Emily's sensory issues and random asthma attacks, Kelly was having a hard time sticking to a schedule, no matter how much she would like it.

Kelly and Oliver had heated disagreements over the best way to manage this stage of life. Oliver wanted Kelly to relax and "go with the flow." In his mind, not everything had to be programmed and preset. This reflected Oliver's natural leaning: relaxed, unstructured, and fairly lenient in his parenting. Kelly, however, found this approach unsettling and chaotic. She never knew how to plan her day, became repeatedly frustrated by her inability to accomplish what she set out to do, and was regularly exhausted when the rest of the family was getting their second wind. She found herself bitter and short-tempered when her family did not conform.

There are formulaic parenting approaches that assert that you will have well-behaved, happier children if they stay on a tight schedule. Because Kelly personally enjoyed this type of lifestyle and routine, she mistakenly believed that it would also benefit the rest of her family. Instead, it was creating tension in the family and frustration for Kelly. She was evaluating her family's home life through a blueprint, an approach, that works well for some homes, but did not benefit Kelly's family.

In counseling, Kelly was able to see the assumptions she had made about how a family should function and the formulaic approach she was applying to their family life. She saw how they were working to the detriment of Oliver and the children. She committed herself to learn how to wisely love her family, and to consider the ways her children (and husband) were wired and the specific needs they each had. Both Kelly and Oliver had natural leanings that needed to be considered, along with the needs of their children that stretched them outside their parenting preferences. Oliver began to realize that the needs of his daughter and his wife might require him to engage and assist in new ways. Kelly and Oliver began adapting their home life accordingly.

Since Oliver was a night owl, he committed to being the parent who was "on" for their daughter at night. He would be responsible for the evening routines of baths, reading, and tucking into bed. Should Emily wake up, have trouble sleeping, or struggle with her breathing, Oliver would handle it. Kelly could prepare for the next day and get to bed at a reasonable hour. She found that if she could get a solid six or seven hours of sleep, she was able to function better, think more clearly, and more easily manage the irregular schedule throughout the day.

The more Kelly thought through how she could love the family God had given her, the more she desired to sacrifice her own preferences for their benefit. She held her agenda and daily plans more loosely and trusted God to give her the grace and energy she needed. As she focused on the needs of her home, she was able to experience contentment even in the midst of chaotic moments. She also understood that she could find ways to thrive in the midst of a family that did not conform to her own personal strengths, weaknesses, and preferences. With the help of Oliver and some wise friends, she found ways to have uninterrupted time alone—thanks to babysitters or kind church members who offered to watch the kids. She got creative in planning simple meals and organized tasks around Emily's naps. She gave herself permission to let some of her perfectionistic standards go.

Likewise, Oliver was stretched yet pleased by the changes they made. Kelly took the early morning shift if Emily woke up. Kelly took charge of the morning routines, getting the children up and ready for the day's activities. Oliver, not being a morning person, was able to sleep in longer and get himself up and out the door on time for work. Though he missed his free evenings, he delighted to see how much more rested and tranquil Kelly had become. Life was busy, but they had established routines that they both embraced, and they treasured the result. Both parents worked together to understand what following Christ looked like in their home, identifying the needs of their children, helping each other thrive, and establishing a home life that they all could embrace.

Parenting according to the needs of the family sometimes goes against our personal parenting preferences, the things we've assumed are basic ground rules for raising children, or our ideal of a model home life. Parenting with your specific family in mind does not mean that you compromise biblical truth, but it means that you contextualize it to your home. It requires a willingness to challenge fixed ideas on how godly family life works.

You Are Your Child's Wise Counselor

God has established you as your child's counselor, educator, discipler, and mentor. As a parent, you are perfectly positioned for this task. Although outside help and professionals can be useful, you are the expert. Very few people in your child's life will be as committed as you are to knowing and understanding them. You spend the most time and energy with your child. You have more conversations and share more of everyday life with your children than anyone else does. You intuitively read their faces, body language, and silences. You sense when something is amiss.

One of our kids always gets a "caught" look when he does something wrong. His face always gives it away when he is lying. Thankfully, he has never figured out what that look is! We can ask him a question and the look will follow. Not all kids are so obvious, but parents can still pick up on subtle cues. Your instincts kick in to tell you when they are hiding something, or hurting, or acting out of character. For example, your daughter comes home and does not make eye contact. She says that her day was fine, heads to her room, and shuts the door. This may be a typical pattern for some children, but for this child, it signals that things are askew. You notice and pursue your daughter. When she shuts down your attempt at conversation, you file away the moment in hopes that the Lord will provide insight or opportunity at a later time.

This understanding does not come from some mystical psychic power. It is discernment honed by years of observation about how your child is wired and her typical responses. Your insights come from thousands of big and small events as you have watched your children handle sadness, fear, anger, hurt feelings, and temptation.

You are already an expert at knowing your children in ways that would take a professional counselor months to figure out. Sometimes parents simply need to slow down enough to evaluate and piece together what we know and perceive. As a counselor, when I talk through circumstances with parents, I often find that their perceptions are accurate. Many parents question their instincts, wondering why they feel strongly about something and whether they are wrong. No doubt any good parent should be open to asking those questions. However, as I draw out why parents feel a certain way, facts and details often emerge that support their conclusions. They've just never taken the time to untangle their thoughts and perceptions.

The Role of the Spirit of God

Parenting must be done in dependence on the Spirit of God. The Spirit equips us for all that God calls us to. He empowers us to be what we need to be for our family and to be Christlike in our parenting. In the book of Acts, we see that after the outpouring of the Holy Spirit, believers were able to give their belongings selflessly, to fellowship together over meals, and to help each other in their time of need. Is this not what we are aiming for? We bear witness to the life of Christ within us when we live by the Spirit.

The Spirit gives discernment and guidance in difficult child-rearing moments. Romans 8:26 tells us that the Spirit of God "intercedes for us with groanings too deep for words." There are times when we feel lost in parenting. We struggle to know what our child needs and how to respond wisely. In those moments, the Spirit intercedes on our behalf. No matter how lost you might feel in those moments, you are not on your own. You have the Spirit of God to help you through.

The Spirit gives direction. Perhaps you have had a subtle nudging in your spirit that gave you pause or made you check into something your child was doing. Parents call this many things: a sixth sense, a gut reaction, a mother's intuition, a response to a multitude of minor irregularities, small glances, or abnormal responses. We also know it to be God's Spirit at work in us. Romans 8:14 says, "For all who are led by the Spirit of God are sons of God." If you are a child of God, you have access to the guidance of the Holy Spirit. When we are struggling to know what our child needs, we can trust the Spirit to grant guidance.

As a parent, God has put you in the unique position of being your child's wise counselor. You have years of experience and interactions that shape what you know. Of course, we can be wrong, blind to things, or misperceive, but when we are committed to knowing our children, praying for wisdom, and open to input from others, we are more than likely to be their best-equipped advocate.

Freedom from formulas does not mean that we can parent however we want. It is quite the opposite. Being free from formulas means that we have to roll up our parental sleeves and do the hard work of understanding our children as unique individuals. And it means asking God for wisdom on how to best apply biblical wisdom to our unique child. Every day you have to ask for God's help, insight, and wisdom. Every day we are to live sacrificially to serve the needs of our family.

We Are Personally Known

Before you become completely overwhelmed by all this, remember that we have a heavenly Father who knows us personally, intimately, and completely. He created us, formed us, and knows what goes on in our hearts better than we know it ourselves. He can go places inside our heads and hearts that no one else can reach, and he meets us there.

Psalm 139 expresses this reality in verses 1–5:

O Lord, you have searched me and known me! You know when I sit down and when I rise up; you discern my thoughts from afar. You search out my path and my lying down and are acquainted with all my ways. Even before a word is on my tongue, behold, O Lord, you know it altogether. You hem me in, behind and before, and lay your hand upon me.

Verses 13–18 go on to describe how well he knows us:

For you formed my inward parts; you knitted me together in my mother's womb. I praise you, for I am fearfully and wonderfully made. Wonderful are your works; my soul knows it very well. My frame was not hidden from you, when I was being made in secret, intricately woven in the depths of the earth. Your eyes saw my unformed substance; in your book were written every one of them, the days that were formed for me, when as yet there were none of them. How precious to me are your thoughts, O God! How vast is the sum of them! If I would count them, they are more than the sand. I awake, and I am still with you.

God the Creator, by his nature, is all-knowing and intimately acquainted with all he has made. We are often tempted to see him as an impersonal force, detached and uninvolved. He is more personal and intimate than we can imagine. We are crafted in his image, known deeply and personally.

Just as we are known intimately by God and guided by him, so we are to know and guide our children. We want our children to feel known and understood. We want the guidance we give them to be personal and specific. We want to bring Scripture to life for them, that they may be drawn to their Creator and his ways.

There are biblical realities that inform your parenting: what is wise, godly, loving, biblical, and God-oriented in our discipline and good stewardship. These truths are found in Scripture, but their application can vary from home to home. The way we go about imparting these qualities to our children or the ways our children learn them may vary but all seek to produce the same result. God gives us freedom to evaluate our home, know our children intimately, discern their needs well, and apply biblical principles with a godly, thoughtful approach.

Becoming an Expert on Your Children

Becoming an expert on my family means that I need to study them. I need to know my spouse well—his strengths, weaknesses, gifts, interests, limitations, and temptations—and look for godly ways to speak, nurture, and balance when needed. We consider each other's parenting styles and how we complement or contradict each other. We consider who tends to handle particular children or certain situations better. For example, Greg is known to be the one who handles vomit and all other bodily fluids in our home. Why? Because the other parent (me) is known to be a wimp. The sight of such things will likely add more vomit to the situation. It is important to take time to know well the people God has placed in your family and to understand how you all function, thrive, and grow together.

The same is true for your child. No one will be as committed to knowing your child as much as you. Counselors, mentors, professionals, and their knowledge will pale in comparison to what you know about your child. When parents are committed to understanding their kids, they know things that seem intuitive, but actually come from years of observing and interacting with their children.

Consider using the following picture to help you understand and know your child better:

Figure 1.
Your Child as a Puzzle

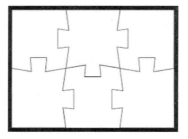

Imagine dumping out the pieces of a puzzle onto a table, though you have no idea what the finished picture is—only a vague sense of what it might become. This is often what we experience with our children, and it can feel a bit overwhelming. All of the pieces are there before you, but the completed picture is by no means clear right away. Early on, we can find the obvious corners and straight lines and begin building a framework for what is yet to unfold. We see glimpses of who our child is becoming, but we do not yet know how all of the pieces will fit together.

You often hear parents say that they saw their child's temperament emerge from the moment they entered the world. "She was strong-willed out of the womb" or "He has been calm and mellow since he was a baby," some parents say. We get snapshots of our children's natural wiring early on, but they are developing. We have an understanding of human nature, sin, individual dispositions and personalities, but we do not yet know how they connect or how they will shape our child's actions.

There are many pieces of the puzzle and we pick them up one by one, examine them, and try fitting them together. At different points, we pick up pieces that look as if they fit, only to find out down the road, when we find a better match, that they really did not go together. As our children develop, we get glimpses of why they do what they do, where they are developmentally, who they are, and what motivates them. We start putting the pieces together. Only time, wisdom, and a commitment to knowing someone deeply will ensure an accurate, meaningful "knowing."

We want to excel at knowing our own children. As Christ knows us intimately, so we strive to intimately know each of our children. Christ knows us by name. He knows our every thought; he sees past our behavior and knows what motivates us. We can't read our children's minds and hearts, but we can be skillful in observing their behaviors, adept in reading what motivates them in situation after situation, proficient in seeing their gifts, weaknesses, aptitudes, fears and insecurities, wise in knowing how to speak hope into their experiences, and committed to wooing them to a personal God.

It is not enough that we commit to knowing them well. We also want to help them know themselves. We want them to grow in understanding their own heart, their motives, their temptations and tendencies, their strengths, weaknesses, aptitudes, giftedness. We want children to know themselves, to know how to live well before God, and to trust him as Savior, Lord, and helper.

Children are not born blank slates. They come with inborn personalities, aptitudes, gifts, tendencies, struggles, disabilities, temperamental strengths and weaknesses. We must seek to identify them in our kids and consider how this should affect the way we parent them. It gives us insight into their spiritual needs and motivations. This then shapes the way we disciple them.

Our son AJ is logical, methodical, and a verbal processor by nature. From the time he was little, whatever was going on in his head came out of his mouth. In his squeaky four-year-old voice, he would say dozens of times a day, "I have to tell you something" or "Can I ask you a question?" Daily, I heard that more times than I can count. As an introvert, I valued quiet. AJ's natural disposition rubbed up against mine in ways that meant I had to learn to sacrifice my comfort to nurture him.

I also discovered that he sometimes talked just to hear himself talk. He would ask a question, only to answer it himself and state why he came to that conclusion. There were times I could have left the room and he might not have noticed because he was carrying on the conversation without me. AJ needed to learn what edifying communication looked like—to be quick to listen and slow to speak. He needed to learn that loving others meant considering if what he had to share was helpful. We began asking him if what was coming out of his mouth was a blessing or an annoyance. Did it build up or tear down—or puff himself up? We were learning as parents to discern the ways that AJ had been created, and where his inclinations might lead him to transgress.

AJ is now fourteen and no longer says 100 times a day, "Can I ask you a question?" But he is still a verbal processor, thinks about life, and enjoys talking about the consequential and inconsequential alike. He enjoys taking a viewpoint and seeing it from various angles. In conversation he sometimes takes the opposite side of an argument just because it is fun for him to consider. There were times when I felt that his desire to debate was defiant or intentionally antagonistic. But knowing him well meant that I put aside my frustrations with what felt like ridiculous discussions and considered his intentions. At other times, wisdom meant that I helped him to see that, though he may be enjoying the debate, others might find it unpleasant. In both instances, the ways I spoke into his life varied, but my intention was the same: to know and love him well.

AJ has grown in maturity, though the same temptations remain for him. He will catch himself when he realizes that what he was about to say might not be helpful or received well. Our role as parents is to help shape, not change, who he is before the Lord, and to help him know himself before the Lord. AJ will always be AJ. We don't want to try to make him into a mini-version of ourselves, but to shepherd him to be all God designed him to be: a godly AJ.

We have six children. None of them are alike. They all think differently, face unique struggles, and express themselves in distinct ways. They enjoy different tastes, styles, and hobbies. They are diverse in the temptations and sinful tendencies they battle. Imagine the work it takes to commit to knowing each one well, and to discipline them to know themselves well before the Lord. Perhaps you do not need to imagine because you are in the same boat! The task is demanding, calling for tremendous wisdom, discernment, effort, and commitment. No wonder formulas are so tempting! We want something simple, straightforward, and uncomplicated.

Our parenting task requires us to:

1. Pursue Christlikeness, being committed to godly character in our own life and before our family.
2. Faithfully seek to establish a home built on Christ.
3. Know our spouse and our children deeply, while helping them to know themselves before the Lord and seeking their personal good above our own.

If we don't embrace this approach, we will revert either to our own natural parenting style (be it good or bad) or to other methods—a cookie-cutter approach. But when forced into a mold, our kids find themselves stifled rather than freed to be who they were created to be. We must work hard to influence them in the ways of God for their benefit but not our own personal gain.

We are all made in the image of God, created to reflect his likeness. We are also made individually, creatively, and uniquely. We all are impacted by sin and wrestle with a fallen nature. We also were created with unique traits and gifts, likes and dislikes, a distinctive built-in innate wiring that makes us who we are. The way we were created leads us in certain directions with particular inclinations, including things like being an introvert or extrovert, tendencies toward leadership or passivity, being loud or quiet, neat and orderly or messy. We are granted gifts and sometimes disabilities to varying degrees.

Children Are Moral Responders

Our kids have hearts that are always active and dynamic. They have hearts that are driven by wants, motives, desires, and agendas. There is nothing passive about any of this! We see in Scripture that, throughout history, people have sought to create substitutes for God. Human beings are often tempted to exchange the Creator for the created thing—to establish mini-gods that are more to our liking. We think they will serve us better.

The Bible tells us that anything we use to replace God becomes an idol (Exodus 20:3–6). Anything at all—even a good thing—can become an idol in our life. It might be relationships, marriage, children, careers, food, or materialism. Our children, likewise, will find themselves looking to find meaning and value apart from God. They will look for things to give them purpose, pleasure, and hope. Throughout Scripture, we see individuals looking for something besides God to satisfy them. Our children may look toward peers, possessions, pleasure (illegal or innocent), appearance, skills, athletics, music, or romance, forgetting their first love, their Creator.

We have hearts that are made to worship. What are your children tempted to worship? From toddlers who want attention, toys, and technology to teens who are looking for identity in peers, sex, addictive substances, body image, or performance, each child will battle with his own heart, which is prone to wander. We want to walk alongside them in this battle, sympathizing, encouraging, providing insight, and pointing them to Christ.

Parents often wrestle with whether they are dealing with a sin issue or a physical/ temperamental strength or weakness. Often it is both. Children do not know what to do with their inattention, forgetfulness, or social awkwardness, so they will often compensate in sinful ways. Having a strong biblical framework for understanding your children helps. You must look at the child as a whole, both the spiritual and the physical. If you ignore the spiritual need for faith and obedience, sin will be excused as "this is just who I am." If you ignore weakness and individual differences, you make temperamental weaknesses into character issues and condemn your children. The danger is that they begin to believe that God condemns them too. We want them to learn greater reliance on a God whose strength is made perfect in weakness.

We all have significant events in our personal histories: things like sufferings, blessings, trauma, the loss of a parent, adoption, constant lifestyle upheaval, growing up in a large or small family, disability, living in poverty or wealth. These things impact the way children see relationships, the world, and themselves. Left to themselves, they will try to make sense out of these experiences but do so inaccurately.

Children interpret life and experiences, whether or not we talk with them about it. We make a mistake when we avoid discussing what we don't want to deal with, thinking that children will not think about it either. Children already are thinking, interpreting, and drawing conclusions about their lives—often without any loving parental guidance or redemptive perspective.

A parent's ability to speak redemptively and interpret their child's experiences and struggles is crucial. We want every part of our child's life to be understood in light of the gospel. We want to help our kids see who they are and what they experience in the light of a biblical worldview. Regardless of the struggles or brokenness our children encounter, we want to instill confidence in a Creator who knows them by name, sees their every thought, and knows the number of their days. When children learn to find their identity in Christ, it creates a grid through which they can make sense of life.

To speak to your child at this level requires really, really knowing what makes your children tick—what motivates them, excites them, tempts them, causes them to cry; what they dream about, where they show great aptitude and promise, and where they struggle, demonstrating weakness or disability.

In his book *Parenting: 14 Gospel Principles That Can Radically Change Your Family*, Paul Tripp speaks to the mentality of "ownership parenting." He states, "It operates on this perspective of parenting: *These children belong to me, so I can parent them in the way I see fit.*"[1] He goes on to explain that ownership parenting does not ask, "What does my child need and how is God calling me to respond?" Rather it is "motivated and shaped by what parents want for their children and from their children."

This reminds me of a scene in the movie *The Lord of the Rings: The Return of the King*. Gandalf the wizard has approached Denethor, steward-ruler of the city of Gondor, and implored him to call for aid as the enemy's armies approach. Denethor responds with contempt, for he knows that Gondor's true king and heir is returning with Gandalf to his rightful throne, thereby undermining Denethor's position of authority. Gandalf rebukes him, saying, "Authority is not given to you, Steward, to deny the return of the king!" Denethor responds angrily, "The rule of Gondor is mine! And no others!"[2] As parents, we must remember that we are merely stewards in the lives of our children. We are called to steward our homes well, but in service to our king, with the ultimate goal that our children choose to follow Christ as their king as well.

---

1. Paul David Tripp, *Parenting: 14 Gospel Principles That Can Radically Change Your Family* (Wheaton: Crossway, 2016), 2–3.
2. *The Lord of the Rings: The Return of the King*, directed by Peter Jackson (2003).

Children as Individuals

To develop a wise and biblical understanding of our children, we need a foundational understanding of human nature. My colleague, Mike Emlet, has written extensively about the biblical view (seen below) of man as sinner, sufferer, and saint.[3] It explains that our children are created in the image of God (though it is only the redeeming work of Christ that transforms them into saints). As image bearers, they are born into a broken, fallen world where they will be impacted by suffering and challenging experiences. They are moral responders, doing battle with a sinful nature that is prone to wander from God. This nature corrupts the way they experience life.

Parents have the task of helping their children understand how God creates but the world corrupts. God creates food, sex, relationships, and our own temperaments, but none of this is immune from sin's ability to corrupt them. Shepherding our children includes giving them insight into their hearts. It requires building a redemptive worldview where they can see that God created everything and everything points to him. It calls for speaking, mentoring, and walking alongside them.

Figure 2. Man as Saint, Sinner, and Sufferer

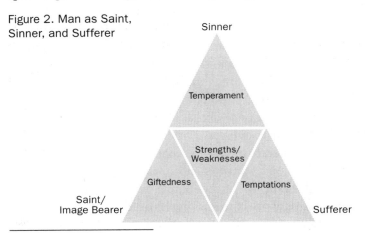

---

3. Michael R. Emlet, *CrossTalk: Where Life & Scripture Meet* (Greensboro, NC: New Growth Press, 2009).

Development

When we start with a biblical understanding of human nature, we can then begin to fill in the puzzle with the individual uniqueness of each child. What makes our children uniquely who they are? And how does Scripture speak into each person's life distinctively?

Isaiah was a twelve-year-old boy who struggled with anxiety. He was physically small for his age, yet spiritually and emotionally mature beyond his years. He developed a keen ability to read people's expressions and perceive attitudes—and potential criticism. He also struggled academically. Reading was difficult for him, which impacted other subjects as he became older. Due to his small size, he was often picked on or overlooked in school. He was sensitive to this and began looking for ways to avoid situations where he might be rejected or chosen last.

Due to his development and academic struggles, many thought he might benefit if he was held back a year in school. He looked like a ten-year-old boy, though he had the maturity and insight of a mature teenager. He enjoyed talking with adults and made friends with older kids outside school. Yet he spent a majority of his day around those with whom he did not fit in. What should parenting Isaiah look like? What does he need?

Isaiah's parents needed help putting together Isaiah's puzzle pieces. They tried to understand what was developmental: what were his physical, temperamental, and academic strengths and weaknesses? What was situational: where did difficult peers, bullying, or wrong educational decisions fit in? Where was Isaiah struggling with poor responses: avoiding social situations, people, and places; hypersensitivity to what others were thinking?

These distinctions are often not clear cut. They often feel obscure and difficult to figure out. Sometimes one struggle appears to cause or connect to another. For example, does Isaiah's delay in physical growth lead to bullying or does his maturity and struggle connecting to his peers lead to his being picked on?

It is not always discernable, but wisdom does the hard work of distinguishing what you can and parenting accordingly.

Isaiah's parents consistently affirmed and nurtured the positive qualities they saw in him, helping him to see his perceptiveness and sensitivity not as a weakness, but as a God-given trait he must learn to steward. They showed compassion as they addressed his anxiety, understanding his struggle while giving him ways to manage the anxious moments. They pointed him to the Lord as his comfort and help, praying for him and with him.

Isaiah's parents knew he needed friends and supports outside of school. They worked on finding him a mentor he could relate to. They got special permission to have him in an older youth group and connected him with one or two mature students they knew would embrace him. School was more difficult to figure out. Isaiah struggled academically and needed extra help. However, they recognized that moving him back a year would not be the solution. It would very likely lead to more difficulty fitting in and a greater sense of discouragement. There was no easy solution. They tried getting him special accommodations, tutoring, and eventually allowed him to be held back, only to have all their concerns validated. Although both parents worked, they eventually pulled him out of school and worked hard to develop an educational program that could fit him.

Isaiah's parents were doing the hard work of understanding their son and seeking to parent him according to his needs. There was trial and error, successes and failures, but they continued to prayerfully seek what was best for him and to ask the Lord for the provision (both personally and materially) to do so.

As parents, we accept that taking good care of our children means keeping up with their physical health. At your child's yearly well check, your doctor measures growth in height, weight, and general health from year to year. This is determined by the typical patterns and norms for your child's age. There are times when a child falls outside the norm on developmental charts but is still healthy. However, the charts indicate what is normative in development and when there is reason for concern.

Our development as human beings involves more than the physical. We develop cognitively, emotionally, socially, and spiritually too. Standard measurements can help us to see when a child is delayed (or gifted) academically and may need specialized services. Tracking someone's development emotionally or socially can indicate whether the child is immature or advanced for his age. In every category, charting a child's development can help us see whether a child is within normal range, advanced, or delayed in a particular dimension of life.

As a counselor, I am trained to consider how a child's development affects his ability to function in age-appropriate settings. Sometimes we miss the fact that a child may meet many developmental milestones for their age but fall significantly short on others, or excel beyond what is normal for their age in still other categories. This can cause significant problems emotionally or socially when a child is forced to conform to what is considered average for their age. This was part of Isaiah's problem.

Parenting well means knowing where your children excel or struggle developmentally and seeking insight as to what would best help them grow. For example, a seven-year-old girl may present as standard or average in physical development and academic achievement, but she may be socially or emotionally behind. Her grades are fairly good and she can keep up in gym class. Yet she struggles to make friends her age, gravitating toward the younger kids at recess and isolating herself from her peers most of the day. As a parent, I might begin by doing everything I can to create opportunities for her to build healthy relationships with children her age. But as time goes on, it becomes obvious that something is still amiss.

What do we do when our children are in some way developmentally behind or ahead of their peer group? We begin by seeking to understand them. We watch for patterns, evaluate what it indicates about the child, and how we need to address them.

The child may be maturing at her own rate; she may simply like younger/older toys and games, or connect with a younger/older peer group. It is just who she is. This requires me as a parent to think creatively about where her most healthy relationships might be found.

When does it help me to accept my child's differences so that I can help her know how to adapt to those differences? When are those differences reflective of something problematic (such as significantly underdeveloped social skills or academic processing issues)? When a weakness impedes daily life or relationships, parents must consider what intervention is advantageous. We have to think about what resources are needed, including professional help, a different environment, special skills, etc. This isn't always immediately clear, but if you as a parent strive to understand your child well, over time you will gain discernment.

In Isaiah's case, it took time and much trial and error, but his parents became students of their son. They reflected on how he was uniquely created, where he was developmentally, what his needs were, and what gifts and aptitudes needed to be developed and encouraged. They became experts at knowing their son and helping him find his identity in who God fashioned him to be. They spoke into the places he struggled with fear, lack of faith, or temptation, and helped him understand his own proclivities. It required them to think outside the box, to look beyond the typical solutions a school district could offer, and to be faithful to understand his heart and struggles well. In doing so, they pointed him to the Lord and parented him wisely.

It is wise to ask when issues are developmental and when they are moral/sin issues. Is this behavior a result of willfulness and sinful desires or just immaturity? Initially, it is not always obvious. But with wisdom, time, and a willingness to engage with a child's struggles, clarity will develop.

Character is about developed traits, moral choices regarding what and who you will become. Temperamental traits are innate qualities, individual tendencies toward being introverted or extroverted, loud or quiet, a follower or leader, dependent or independent, organized or disorganized, etc. That said, there are times when an innate temperamental trait becomes a character issue. For example, a child might struggle greatly with attentiveness and organization (a personal weakness). He doesn't naturally know how to organize, he has a poor memory, or he just doesn't know where to begin with a task. We do not fault him; we help him. However, when he is given skills and resources to help him and he chooses not to apply them, that choice becomes a character issue. The choice may be motivated by laziness over the effort required, or a lack of concern for how it impacts the people around him. It could also be that he avoids attempting what feels insurmountable. No matter what the reason, the child is a moral responder in the choice he makes.

Parenting with a focus on the uniqueness of my family means that my choices about things like discipline and schooling will be based not on my ideals, but on what is loving and helpful to the people God has placed in my home. When my parenting ideals and my children's needs collide, that is when I need the Spirit of God to give wisdom on how to proceed.

Personal conviction and preferences sometimes look the same and may have their virtues. But don't be surprised if the children God grants you clash with those worthy and noble ideals. In that case, be prepared to forego those desires, whatever they may be, and believe that God is inspiring something far better.

You are learning to contextualize Scripture to the family God has blessed you with. Formulas and ideals run aground because we assume that if we plug every child into our formulas, they will all come out as poster children for success. Instead, they are often hindered or harmed. Ask yourself, "Am I becoming discerning at knowing my children?" and "What does godly love look like in the family God gave me?"

Scripture is full of examples of bad family life, more so than model families. There is corruption, the stealing of birthrights, murder between siblings, and incest. Hardly what you and I aspire to! We also see loving relationships, friends that stick closer than brothers, individuals who put the needs of their family above their own—people who exemplify Christlikeness in the way they conduct themselves.

Write your own story for your family, because you are committed to the gospel, to loving the Lord and your family, and to knowing your family well enough to write a story that reflects your uniqueness. The way my husband and I do our family will not be the way you do yours. We are not the ideal. We simply strive to be the ideal *us*—what God calls us to be for our kids and our marriage. Be what God calls *your* family to be.

Parenting Toolbox
Putting the Family Puzzle Together

Take the picture of the empty puzzle and blow it up for each child (perhaps for each parent as well!). Thoughtfully work on labeling each piece with details about each child in a particular aspect of life—interests, gifts, weaknesses, personality, aptitudes, tendencies toward sin, places of struggle, developmental characteristics. Put the pieces together to create a visual of how each child is wired. Perhaps you will move pieces around as you think about how they are each uniquely created. Perhaps you will think of more pieces to add, or change how you see something. But take time to consider each person and how you understand them.

Developmentally, how do your children differ? In what particular areas is each one more mature and less mature? Where do you see your kids struggle with faith? With temptations toward sin? Talk through ways you can speak into their struggle winsomely and with hope.

You must continue to grow in understanding them as they develop and mature. You must also consider how you can inspire them to grow and how you can shepherd them more personally. Where do they need to hear the gospel more clearly? How is it applied more particularly to their struggles? How can you nurture their giftings and strengths? How can you help them see themselves accurately, the way God sees them?

Consider placing every family member's puzzle next to the others. As parents, ask yourselves what insights this exercise gives you into how you should parent your children. What changes would you make? What does it affirm you are doing well?

Reflection Questions

1. What are some ways you parent out of your own disposition and natural preferences? In what ways is that good and helpful? In what ways is it not?
2. What things have you noticed about each of your children that have shaped the way you parent them?
3. Are there things that you are beginning to notice and struggle to know how to address? What are they?
4. What are some of the similarities and differences between your children? How can those things guide your efforts to get to know each of them better?
5. Brainstorm some practical ways to get to know each child better. How would these approaches shape your interactions with them? As you learn more about them, how will that affect the kind of mentoring, discipline, rules, or freedoms that you give them?

CHAPTER 4

Parenting According to the Needs of Your Family

Being an expert at knowing each of our children naturally leads to a commitment to shape our parenting and our homes to serve our family well. This does not mean that life revolves around any one person. Rather, it establishes Christ at the center and then seeks to minister to the individuals and to the family as a whole. It takes into account our personal strengths and weaknesses, our marriage, financial needs, careers, choices in education and extracurricular activities, ministry opportunities, church activities, and, overall, the things that will nurture the family as a whole and the individuals within it. Each decision can feel weighty when you are trying to balance multiple needs. Choices are made knowing that there can be implications for everyone.

I didn't realize it at first, but I had an idealized picture of the type of parent I wanted to be: calm, rational, easy-going, gracious, and wise—a sage in my children's eyes. I wanted the type of relationship where I could sit down and reason with my children about their behavior and choices and win them over with my insight. This is not a bad ideal. However, I quickly came to realize that not all of my children bought into it.

God gave us children with their own opinions, preferences, tastes, and natural proclivities. He gave them aptitudes and gifts that needed to be encouraged and developed. They each came with personal weaknesses that needed to be recognized or compensated for. They are individually prone to areas of temptation and sin, and it was our job to help them see them and point them to Christ in their need. They were all given unique personalities by the Lord. All of that shaped the work of discipleship that Greg and I embarked on as parents.

Parenting by faith and wisdom does not mean that we parent in the way that makes us most comfortable. When we base good parenting on what "feels right" to us, we mistakenly assume that our parenting preferences are what's best for our children, which may or may not be true.

A non-assertive parent may be given a child with disabilities that requires them to be their child's advocate, to be assertive and push back when they know that more help should be offered. Another parent is affectionate and loves to touch, but is given a child who does not enjoy demonstrations of affection. Another child's bent toward fear and anxiety might rub up against a parent who enjoys adventure and risk taking.

A single-parent home, a blended family, or a family where one parent has a significant disability will find that issues of discipline, homework, cooking, etc., will fall to the parent best suited for it (or the only parent). It might mean that parents establish roles that are nontraditional, but suit their gifting and the family's needs. It might mean that the father is the one best suited to be home with the kids after school to help with homework. It may mean that the mother is the primary disciplinarian in a blended family.

You may desperately want to homeschool your children but, due to unexpected life circumstances or the clear needs and disabilities of your child, you find yourself relying on a school system better equipped to assist with your child's educational needs. Sometimes what we fear is settling for less is really God's better plan. We need to be willing to let go of our plan and trust God to provide what is best.

Many of the parents I have counseled do not parent intentionally. Perhaps I should say, they do not intentionally evaluate the needs of the people in the family. Why is this true? Because we all receive help and input in different ways. We all have our own weaknesses, temptations, aptitudes, and disabilities that impact what we need to hear, how we hear it, and why we reject or accept it. We go on autopilot, relying on what we know, on our natural leanings, and on what we learned growing up.

Consider these differences that I have observed in children I have counseled:

- Some children argue or are oppositional/defiant. They need structure and accountability.
- Some children nod their heads yes while silently disagreeing. They need someone to notice and gently call them out.
- Some children are sensitive, with a tendency toward fear. They may shut down. They lack self-awareness and need a patient adult to draw them out and reflect back to them.
- Some children demonstrate developmental delays or impairments that impact how they hear or process information. They need an approach tailor-made to their challenges so that they can learn.
- Some children do not respond to laid-back parenting. They thrive on routines and rhythms. They need to be highly structured and disciplined or they fall into unhealthy or ungodly patterns.
- Some children do not respond well to overly structured households; they need grace and extra time, less pressure to think and accomplish tasks.

In this list, a parent's response should be based on the needs of the child instead of the parent's preferences. Your knowledge of your children can and should shape how you shepherd them, engage with their struggles and weaknesses, address the temptations and sin that entice them, and encourage their strengths, gifting, and spiritual sensitivity.

Picture your son's tendency to hide his feelings or the things that tempt him. Over time, you've seen this tendency; you've observed places in his life where he struggles with peer pressure or the desire to fit in with ungodly individuals. How do you approach him? Do you wait for the next situation to arise? Do you sit him down and go into a lecture that only you will appreciate?

Knowing your son's struggle is only part of the challenge. Now you must pray for discernment in reaching his heart, reflecting back to him what you see and pointing him to Christ.

Becoming a Student of God's Word

Our knowledge of our children, although vitally important, is not all we need to parent wisely. We also need to become students of God's Word. The Bible is the authoritative voice that gives us wisdom and direction as we parent. Scripture guides us in how to live out God's ways within relationships. Think about Paul's words to parents in Ephesians 6:1–4:

> Children, obey your parents in the Lord, for this is right. "Honor your father and mother" (this is the first commandment with a promise), "that it may go well with you and that you may live long in the land." Fathers, do not provoke your children to anger, but bring them up in the discipline and instruction of the Lord.

I meet with many parents who are uncertain about what they should do. Yet here it is plainly laid out for us: parents are to bring up their children in the discipline and instruction of the Lord and not provoke them. Children are called to obey their parents. The details of how these principles are worked out will vary from family to family, according to your children's specific needs. But as we help our children to learn to obey, and think carefully about how to do this without provoking them, we can be confident that we are going in the right direction. Wisdom allows our methods to vary, but our goals will always be similar.

These are the overall principles, but God gives you freedom to apply them specifically and wisely to your family. God's Spirit is there to help you apply the right principle at the right time. Scripture does not always give us specifics on how to help a child in the midst of a temper tantrum, or what to do when your teen struggles with pornography. But it does give us the principles for parenting well (discipleship, discipline, stewardship, guidance, and training), and it helps us to know how to engage relationally in moments of anger, grief, anxiety, and discipline. God's Word also gives us the encouragement to persevere in faithfulness and prayer for our children.

Parenting according to the needs of your family is only possible as we become students of Scripture. Make it your aim to know what the Scripture says about anger, forgiveness, communication, desires, and conflict. This will guide the choices you make in parenting.

For example, many parents struggle to know how to handle conflict in the home. Consider these biblical principles:

- As parents, don't provoke your children to anger or discouragement (Colossians 3:21).
- Look at yourself first and teach your kids to be willing to look at their actions before pointing out another's sin (Matthew 7:5).
- Be quick to listen and slow to speak (James 1:19).
- Demonstrate humility and patience (Ephesians 4:2).
- Be willing to be tender toward them and forgive (Ephesians 4:32).
- Show understanding toward your children and draw them out (Proverbs 20:4).
- When possible, model the ability to overlook an offense (Proverbs 19:11).
- Do not return evil for evil (1 Peter 3:9–11).

- Help them to see their hearts and desires in conflict (James 4:1).
- Consider the needs of others above your own (Philippians 2:3).
- Do what you can to live at peace with each other (Romans 12:18).
- Foster a willingness to confess sin and pray for one another (James 5:16).

If you are wondering how to do this, consider searching the Word of God for stories, examples, and parables that help you better understand how God deals with his people and how he expects us to interact with one another. Surround yourself with other parents who think wisely and have raised children who know the Word of God well.

Start a notebook with verses that you have found on this topic or others. When your child is struggling with anxiety, turn to God's Word for help. How does God speak to us in our fear? What does he tell us to do? How does he meet and comfort us? Ask God to grant you discernment to wisely apply truth to your children's lives. James 1:5 reminds us that when we lack wisdom, God offers to give it to us generously.

Using the Bible, you can teach your children the principles they need to learn to thrive in God's world—empathy, kindness, forgiveness, other-centeredness, a good work ethic—the list goes on. All of these principles are in Scripture, but their application will vary from home to home. The way we go about instilling such qualities in our children and the ways our children learn them will vary, though the goals are the same.

Proactive Instead of Reactive Parenting

Tyler is an energetic and busy nine-year-old. He wakes up going sixty mph and does not stop until his head hits the pillow at night. He rushes through homework, chores, dinner, and most things he is required to do. His parents find this frustrating and, despite their constant reminders, Tyler continues to go at full speed. It is unclear whether his momentum is a result of weakness and impulsivity or willful disobedience. Out of frustration, his parents often punish him in hopes that he will change. Other times, out of the same frustration, they throw their hands up in resignation, accepting the behavior as though it will never change.

Parents often fall on one side or the other. We see weaknesses and challenging patterns in our children's lives as "just who they are" and dismiss the need to teach them self-discipline or healthier behaviors. Or we see challenging behaviors as willful sin and defiance, and choose to respond punitively to force behavioral change (or so we hope!).

But when you combine biblical principles with your intimate knowledge of your child, you are well on your way to becoming a proactive instead of a reactive parent.

Too often we parent reactively, rather than proactively. We wait to have a hard conversation until a child is in trouble. Perhaps your child has a relatively minor struggle like not brushing their teeth, hiding their homework, and/or arguing with their siblings. Or perhaps the problems have escalated to cheating in school, fighting at recess, using inappropriate apps or websites, pornography, sexting, sexually acting out, and/or drugs. Either way, we tend to wait too long to speak into our children's lives. We need to offer them biblical help before they are deep into a struggle or sin pattern, past the point where we can influence the way they think about an issue.

This quote, attributed to Charles Spurgeon, explains the difference between proactive and reactive parenting:

> I heard of a man who said that he did not like to prejudice his boy, so he would not say anything to him about Religion. The devil, however, was quite willing to prejudice the lad, so very early in life he learned to swear, although his father had a foolish and wicked objection to teaching him to pray. If ever you feel it incumbent upon

you not to prejudice a piece of ground by sowing good seed on it, you may rest assured that the weeds will not imitate your impartiality. Where the plow does not go and the seed is not sown, the weeds are sure to multiply. And if children are left untrained, all sorts of evil will spring up in their hearts and lives.

Spurgeon's point is that it is better to actively shape our children; otherwise, the world will do so. We must proactively shape our children's view on any and every subject. It is far better than trying to debunk an inaccurate view. It's better to teach them God's way of living than wait until they have gone their own (wrong) way. Kids need a biblical view of life and the world around them—one that extends to every area of their lives and every issue they might face. If you don't share a biblical perspective with them, someone else will share theirs and you may not like what they have to say. The more we proactively bring them to God's Word while engaging in their world, the more we will equip them to stand up to the temptations and pressures they face.

When we remain silent, they will perceive our silence as indifference, inadequacy, or both. As parents, we have to know what temptations our children face in their school, peer groups, and social media, and then be willing to engage them on all of these issues.

Part of proactive parenting means that we are always paying attention to the subtle patterns that creep into our children's lives or our family's lifestyle. These may be things that don't seem problematic at first and may even be necessary. But when they become habits, they slowly change the dynamics in the home.

For a period of time, my husband and I had differing work schedules that meant that one of us was "single parenting" on any given night of the week. In an effort to survive this phase, I was making quick meals, reaping the benefits of drive-thru and allowing the kids to pray, eat, and do their homework while I tried to accomplish my to-do list. Though necessary for a time, it would have been (and to some degree was becoming) a way to be disconnected from our kids and as a family. It was not our normal dinner routine, nor what we'd want our evening schedule to look like. We were not sitting down together, catching up on each other's lives. It was a phase of "fast-food" relating. It communicated only what was essential to get us through the essentials. However, there was no relational value to it. We were not "connecting," we were simply coexisting. We noticed new patterns emerging that were not healthy for us.

As we became aware what was happening, Greg and I had to make a few decisions. We had to agree that our priority was being with our kids at night. We tried a few options for the short term but then had to make some hard choices to sacrifice things we were doing in order to make our family time a priority. For the long haul, this meant that we would choose not to work in the evening and would rearrange our work schedules. It required taking pay cuts or working at different times to be there for our children. It required saying no to some good opportunities so that I would not miss events that were important to my children. They attended school and we had maybe three hours at night, if we were lucky, to just be with them. Therefore, we made sure that we were home and not committed every night of the week. We also made sure that *they* were not always out and busy every night of the week. We decided to have a no electronics rule during the week (thought exceptions could be made) because we really wanted those three hours to be meaningful. We read aloud, played board games, hung out on our porch to talk, or helped them with homework. We found ways to make dinnertime full of activities and conversation that they would be interested in. (Some are included in the Parenting Toolbox.)

In my counseling, I am concerned to see more and more passivity entering into modern-day parenting. Although I am sure that this is not entirely new, I notice that many parents desire to occupy their kids rather than engage them. Much of the time, they are trying to keep the children busy and involved while they maintain their own busy schedules. The use of electronics makes it very tempting to allow kids to be occupied with their devices for long periods of time. Some parents feel that electronic devices are safe, in-home babysitters. And it might feel as if the children are safer; after all, when they are using an electronic device, they can be home, occupied, and in close proximity to us. We can see them, know what they are doing (we presume), and feel good that they are all spending time at home together. It conveys a false sense of "togetherness."

Every parent knows that there are times when we just need a little peace and quiet; a half an hour or so where the kids are engaged in a game or watching TV so that we can finish a project or cook dinner. These are not the moments I am concerned about. I am talking about the hours spent surfing the internet, watching videos, living on social media, and coming home from school to spend much of their family time in separate rooms absorbed in another world. Even if the whole family is home, there is little interaction, no meaningful conversation, with everyone essentially living in their own world within the same building.

As parents, we are tempted to allow this. It is easier and seems benign, but this is not proactive parenting. Instead of getting to know our children, we are letting them drift away. Instead of teaching them biblical principles that will help them live kindly and wisely, we are letting them live in a world of their own with most of the input from their peers, not their parents.

You Have a Helper

As you read this chapter, you might be feeling a bit discouraged and burdened by everything there is to do. Know your child! Know the Bible! Be proactive! Sounds like a lot, doesn't it? If only Scripture spelled out what to do when your child was having anxiety over getting on the bus, or when your son has been shown pornography on his friend's phone. All of a sudden, Scripture begins to feel vague and impractical to our current struggle. Don't believe it! Wisdom is available and you are not alone. You have a Helper, the living God, to guide you and your family.

Far too often we rely on our own grit and determination to parent well. How often do we get discouraged by our lack of patience, quick temper, frustration, moments of giving in to what is easiest, rather than what is beneficial and needed in the moment? That's a daily occurrence in our home.

It seems simple, even obvious, that a Christian would depend on God for all of life, especially for the hard job of parenting. Yet often we try to function without relying on God for wisdom, help, and power. We perform within our own abilities, giving little thought to how Christ would play a part in the moment. We respond to conflict, discipline, homework, life choices, and serious family conversations without even thinking about God or asking for his help.

How would it change our parenting if we were confident in God's ability to work within us and give us the resources we need to love, discipline, and parent well? As you think about how you approach parenting, take to heart what Moses said to Joshua as he faced the impossible task of leading God's people to the Promised Land:

> "Be strong and courageous, for you shall go with this people into the land that the LORD has sworn to their fathers to give them, and you shall put them in possession of it. It is the LORD who goes before you. He will be with you; he will not leave you or forsake you. Do not fear or be dismayed." (Deuteronomy 31:7–8)

Those words are also for us as we parent. You and I are not in this alone. The Spirit of God is at work and intimately involved in our parenting. There will be times when we do not know what to do or how to respond. In the moments when we feel confused, lost, or heartbroken, we can trust that the Spirit will intercede for us and direct us.

75

Mitch and Camille found parenting their thirteen-year-old son very taxing. He was strong-willed, often defiant, and prone to argue about every request they made of him. He bickered with his siblings, maneuvered for his own agenda, and turned peaceful family moments into battlegrounds. Their desire for a happy, peaceful family was compromised by their son's spitefulness.

Their natural preference for rational, engaging conversations did not work with him and they found interacting with him exhausting and discouraging. Loving their son well often meant stricter enforcement of consequences. It meant staying on top of infractions and setting aside their desire for peace in order to engage calmly and consistently with his petulance. It meant redefining what good parenting looked like with a challenging temperament, whether it was for a season of their son's life or for the long haul.

There was no blueprint, but they sought the Lord for wisdom as they created their own. They confessed their own failures, learned to respond more calmly but firmly, and prayed more for their child. They had to establish rules and check-ins, regularly following up on where he was and what he was doing. They had to consider how to address behavior, moods, and attitudes on a daily basis, while reminding themselves to affirm their love for him. They learned to navigate their son's anger and not sin with their own. They relied on the Lord for the perseverance and fortitude they needed day by day.

They also had to shield their other children from their son's volatile moments, and make sure they were not depriving his younger siblings of parental time and energy. They regularly felt poured out, wondering what they would have left for the next day. But they would wake up trusting their Helper to give them what they needed. Sometimes parents face these challenges for a season or a stage in the child's life; others find that this is their parenting experience for the child's whole life, and they learn what long-suffering, persevering love requires.

God certainly knew that our children would have parents with strengths, weaknesses, needs, struggles, and natural inclinations of our own. It isn't an accident that you were designated as your child's parent. In God's wisdom, he matched children and parents, knowing that our personalities and proclivities would be at odds with one another at times. He not only knew it, he designed it. These divinely-created differences enrich our relationship with each other. We become iron sharpening iron (Proverbs 27:17). We also grow to have the mindset of Christ. A fragrant offering flows out of those who sacrifice personal rights for the interests of others (Philippians 2:3–7). He also will empower you for the mission.

Your family is to be distinctive. God gave you his Word to guide you and his Spirit to empower you. Begin thinking about what it means to establish your home based on the people God has put in your family.

Parenting Tool Box
Encouraging Mealtime Conversations

Here are some ways you can foster conversation with your children at meals:

1. Conversation Starters: There are many good resources available to get children and teens talking beyond the "How was your day?" type of interaction. Some conversation starters come in boxes to sit on your table or in your kitchen to pull out anytime you want. Search online for conversation starters. There are also apps for your phone to use anytime and anywhere you go.
2. Discourage technology over meals (including Mom and Dad!). Model face-to-face conversations that value knowing and being known by one another.
3. There are fun, sometimes goofy games you can play around the table that require repeating what others

have said. You might play I Spy, or "I'm thinking of an animal." When you have young children, you are connecting, being playful, and teaching them to think and talk. Ironically, our teenagers become equally engrossed—even if it is only because they want to win.

4. "Agree/ Disagree." We began this years ago to engage our kids in valuable discussions. It would start with one of us saying, "Agree or Disagree? Secrets are good." Then everyone would go around the table and share whether they agreed or disagreed and defend their position (or explain why). This is beneficial for several reasons: (a) It gave our kids freedom to disagree with us in healthy ways. (b) It forced them to think, to come up with reasons for what they thought and believed. (c) They benefited from a group conversation with people who had differing views. (d) It gave us the ability to bring up really tough topics to talk about with them.

Reflection Questions

1. Once you feel that you know the needs of your family members, how do you begin shaping family life? What might it look like in your home?

2. What tend to be your parenting preferences? Do your preferences help or hinder your parenting? Does this vary from child to child?

3. Where do you feel stretched beyond your abilities with your children? How do you tend to respond?

4. What is the difference between proactive and reactive parenting? Where do you see the tendency to be reactive with your children?

5. Do you find that you struggle more with one child than another? Can you identify what makes it challenging for you?

CHAPTER 5

When Rules Are Broken

If parents carry [discipline] lovingly towards their children, mixing their mercies with loving rebukes, and their loving rebukes with fatherly and motherly compassions, they are more likely to save their children than being churlish and severe towards them. —John Bunyan[1]

When your son is regularly lying or your daughter is screaming hateful things, be aware of your first reaction. For many of us, it is to retaliate. "You're not going to talk to me that way!" Perhaps you raise your voice in return or respond in anger. Maybe your temptation is to give in, emotionally shut down, or check out. Either way, responding out of your instincts often leads to bad responses that don't address your child's real problem.

Regardless of where your parental tendencies lie, it's easy to make the mistake of thinking that punishment or discipline is what changes character. It certainly impacts it. It aids in addressing behavior and character, and demonstrates the natural consequences and repercussions of misbehavior. However, it is not the driving influence behind good character, nor should we want it to be.

---

1. John Bunyan, *The Life and Death of Mr. Badman* (1680), Acacia John Bunyan Online Library, http://acacia.pair.com/Acacia.John.Bunyan.

In the church, there are many heated debates about the type of discipline children require. I don't wish to enter into them except to say this: We can lose sight of the forest for the trees. Throughout Scripture, the goal of discipline is to teach Christlike character, self-discipline, stewardship, self-control, a good work ethic, and service . . . and love for God and man.

Consider some of the following principles we read about in Scripture:

Principles of Discipline

1. Obedience and discipline are meant to be life-giving (Ephesians 6:1–4). When we love God's ways, we learn that living within the boundaries God has given us protects us and allows us to flourish.
2. A hallmark of discipline is love (Proverbs 3:12; 13:24; Hebrews 12:5–6).
3. A hallmark of Christlikeness is discipline (Deuteronomy 8:5; Hebrews 12:6–7; Proverbs 3:12).
4. Discipline brings delight and fruit to the life of the one who receives it (Proverbs 29:17; Hebrews 12:11).
5. Discipline, rebuke, and correction all lead to righteousness (2 Timothy 3:16–17).
6. Children left to themselves bring shame, reproof, and foolishness (Proverbs 29:15; 12:1).
7. Correction and discipline should be done with gentleness and patience (Galatians 6:1).
8. Parents should never embitter or discourage their children (Ephesians 6:4; Colossians 3:21).

Parental discipline should be merciful and loving, while instilling self-discipline and a disciplined life in our kids. It should produce a desire for the Christlike life, not a fear of punishment (or of the punisher). It is a discipline that generates a strength of mind and heart toward the things of God. It does what it does for the sake of the receiver (the child), not for what the parent might receive in return, even though there is a fruitfulness associated with godly parenting.

Discipline is never intended primarily for the benefit of a parent or adult; it is not for the sake of a comfortable home life or ease. Your children's behavior was never meant to be a mark of success, a medal or jewel on your parenting crown. Rather, it exists to help our children become wise. Our children notice when we discipline in anger because we have been inconvenienced, or because we are trying to force our own agenda. They sense when our rule setting, correction, or rebuke is for their well-being. Not only is it noticeable to them, it is easier for them to accept.

Disciplining your children may create anxiety for you. You fear your child's anger or rejection. Your desire for your child's love and acceptance keeps you from doing what is most loving— instruction and correction. When I genuinely care for and delight in my children, I am willing to do the uncomfortable work of discipline.

We Are All Wandering Sheep

A Christ-centered home is not the picture of an idyllic family with perfect parents and obedient kids in a happy and tranquil home. Quite the opposite. It is a home filled with wandering sheep in need of a good Shepherd. It is a home full of broken, imperfect people, who see their need for help, forgiveness, and grace. Humility and a shared need of a Savior are hallmarks of a Christ-centered home. Our kids can trust our correction more when they see our need for it as well. They accept input better when they see us humble ourselves.

Young people are more vulnerable when they see that we are unpretentious and vulnerable ourselves. When I work hard to establish relationship with my kids, they are open to hearing correction. I find that they often secretly yearn for it. But rules without connection and rapport result in children who see their parents (and Christ) as distant, authoritarian, unloving, and impersonal. The reverse may be true as well: kids who have parents who want to be their best friends but draw no boundaries wonder if the parent cares what happens to them. Kids instinctively sense that a parent who doesn't give them rules does not love them. I've heard teens say this in counseling many times. They push the limits just to see if their parents will step in.

Anger in Parents

A fool gives full vent to his anger. (Proverbs 29:11 CSB)

Anger in parents is a grace killer in your home. Anger in parenting can stem from a variety of personal agendas, when parents seek compliance, obedience, personal comfort, respect, the good opinion of others, reputation, etc. What we know is that angry responses in parenting are never about a love and concern for a child.

Here are some things that anger does in parenting:

- Anger instills in a child a fear of a person rather than a fear of God. It incites animosity rather than trust.
- Anger teaches children that any sin and failure will cause hostility from God. They worry that God responds to them in similar ways.
- Anger crushes your children's spirit. They feel shame and worldly guilt instead of life-giving faith that produces change. It produces condemnation, not conviction.
- Anger embitters your children and alienates them from you and possibly other adults.

You can combat this by reining in your own emotions so that anger, fear, and frustration do not control your discipline. Don't be easily offended. Though it is right for kids to know that their words can impact you, we do not want to hold them hostage to our emotional irregularities or insecurity. Invite feedback and critiques from your children. Let them say the hard things they need to say to you. Ask how things felt to them. Ask what you could have said or done to help them in the moment. Pray with them and for them. We should pray that we are not a stumbling block to our children, but a pathway to hope and the good news.

Forgiveness Is Essential

Developing children who can take an honest look at themselves and confess their sin and failure requires a home that makes forgiveness a value. This cannot be manufactured in an artificial way. It can't simply be a rote procedure kids are taught, though they do need to be taught what forgiveness is and isn't. Once they are taught, it must then be nurtured in an atmosphere of grace that is practiced generously in family relationships. It becomes the air you breathe in your home; you love, you admonish, you forgive as Christ forgave you. It is the fragrant offering of Christ to those around us.

Forgiveness is an essential quality in a home. Children will sin. Parents sin. We all fail and make poor choices. Our children will at times shock us, disappoint us, and hurt us. We will have an opportunity to help them grow through it. If your children approach you with their mistakes, will you be quick to condemn? To lecture? Or to love and forgive? How would your children answer this question: *When I make mistakes and fail, my parents* _____. If you desire a family that models Christ, you must exhibit belonging, acceptance, kindness, and compassion as you demonstrate forgiveness.

In considering discipline, it is important to discern when things can be overlooked and when things must be addressed. Do I demonstrate to my children a willingness to overlook things that are not intentional? Do I look for moments when I can extend grace so they see God's compassion? Will I berate them for a mistake or simply offer kindness? Proverbs 19:11 says, "Good sense makes one slow to anger, and it is his glory to overlook an offense."

When children have gracious parents, they may fear disappointing them, but they do not fear their wrath. They know they can approach them because they demonstrate compassion even in their discipline. They personify 1 Peter 4:8: "Love covers a multitude of sins" and reveal Christ's life within them. This becomes a powerful attraction for children, something they want to understand and ultimately follow.

Parents who are approachable and humble, willing to overlook an offense, and giving others the benefit of doubt help produce wise, mature young people. These qualities strengthen the parent-child relationship, as well as a child's trust in parental authority and leadership.

Assessing Your Family Rules

What rules do you have for your family? When I ask this in counseling, most parents say something like this: "We really don't have too many: be nice, do your homework, be home by 10:00 p.m., etc." When prodded further, the list begins to grow with rules like: don't leave the toothpaste on the counter, no technology in your bedroom, keep your room clean, the family cat is not allowed in your room, etc.

All families need rules. Rules in school, home, work, and life help establish order and maintain safety. They provide instruction and help us discern wise practices. Deuteronomy 6 starts off this way: "Now this is the commandment—the statutes and the rules—that the LORD your God commanded me to teach you, that you may do them in the land to which you are going over, to possess it" (v. 1). Over and over again in Scripture, God relays his statutes to his chosen leaders and prophets, so that his people might know how to live, remain safe, and relate to one another. His statutes also reveal who he is. God's statutes and rules point back to his character and his ways so that we may love him more deeply and follow him. The passage goes on to say:

"Hear, O Israel: The LORD our God, the LORD is one. You shall love the LORD your God with all your heart and with all your soul and with all your might. And these words that I command you today shall be on your heart. You shall teach them diligently to your children, and shall talk of them when you sit in your house, and when you walk by the way, and when you lie down, and when you rise. You shall bind them as a sign on your hand, and they shall be as frontlets between your eyes. You shall write them on the doorposts of your house and on your gates." (Deuteronomy 6:4–9)

In this passage, we are called to take every opportunity to point our kids to the Lord in daily living, to walk with them, talk with them, live it out, and establish it in our homes.

We are given freedom in how we establish rules in our family. However, even our rules serve a larger purpose to varying degrees. The question is, Why do your rules exist? We can be very pragmatic and shortsighted when rules first develop. We see a problem and we fix it with a rule. Shoes are strewn all over the house, therefore new rule: shoes only go in the sunroom. The TV is too loud? New rule: sound on the TV cannot go beyond volume level 15, or the TV stays off. Such rules are not necessarily bad, but the problem is that they are always established in reaction to inconveniences or problems. We want to consider the big picture: How does this rule affect everyone? What are the reasons for or against it? Can it be maintained? Does it maintain harmony or cause relational conflict? Do rules always primarily serve one person's comfort and convenience? Are they for your comfort and convenience or for your child's benefit?

There are many good reasons to have rules. Some rules simply help keep the home running—who takes the dog out, when people take showers, who has what chores, when laundry can be done, carrying your dishes to the sink, eating (or not) on the couch, taking your shoes off at the door. These rules are not based on a moral principle. They are functional. They are practical, serve the entire home, and require everyone's participation. Such rules can evolve over time to reflect the changing needs and structure of the family.

Then there are rules that instill good hygiene, healthy habits, and good practices: brushing your teeth, using deodorant, not picking your nose, picking up your room, making your bed, doing homework at a regular time or place, studying without the TV on, etc. Such rules are for the benefit of our children. When emphasized earlier in a child's life, they become habits as the child grows.

Other rules are meant to instill good character and teach God's ways: how we speak to another, what language is acceptable, rules about giving, honesty, serving, stewarding our time, technology use, and money. From home to home, parents vary on issues like stewardship, healthy technology use, or acceptable speech.

We often have rules that flow out of strong personal values. These are not wrong necessarily; you just have to know where they come from. Sometimes these rules flow out of what we, as parents, feel is a priority or calling for our home life: community service or volunteering, missions, serving as a foster home, or taking in refugees. Such callings carry with them the need for certain implicit rules, like helping people feel safe and welcomed, and a willing attitude to serve. Sometimes the rules are very explicit. For example, foster homes are required to comply with certain regulations, and social workers enforce those rules. A home in which a parent or child has a disability, sensory issues, or medical needs will establish rules that address those needs and everyone must adapt to them.

Families develop different rules about technology, homework, dating, and so on. There is freedom here to establish rules based on the uniqueness of your family. The rules would reflect things like a parent's conscience, a parent's ability to manage a certain schedule, a child's ability to handle responsibility and freedom, the gifts you hope to nurture in your children, and any weaknesses or needs that require focused help.

Rules of any kind can be developed for countless reasons. The challenge is to make sure the reasons are good. Be clear about why the rules are there and how they are meant to benefit the family. Be clear that some rules are not moral issues; they are there simply to help bring order and sanity to the family. Kids benefit when such things are explained to them instead of being told, "Because I said so, that's why." It helps them to know that we see the difference between morally-based rules and rules that simply serve a functional purpose.

Consequences

I've heard many parents say, "We've exhausted all options, all approaches, all kinds of consequences, and nothing has worked. I tried being calm. I tried consistent discipline. I tried appealing to my child's conscience and praying with and for my child. Nothing has helped."

What parents often mean is that their efforts did not produce the desired change in behavior or attitude. The assumption is that if we do all the "right things," our kids will do the same. A formula was applied but it proved useless.

As we have seen, kids are moral responders. They choose whether and how they will embrace our instruction. Children do not come to us as blank slates. They come with their own personalities and temptations toward particular sin. Of course, the way you parent adds another significant factor, but to assume that good parenting will produce well-behaved children incorrectly places all the responsibility for the outcome solely on you.

That said, we should consider whether a particular consequence for a particular child has a helpful impact or whether it is potentially harmful. Harmful could mean it crushes their spirit, embitters them toward authority, and is oppressive or unrealistic. Harmful could mean it has no impact at all, which then emboldens a child's poor behavior. We must always evaluate the effect that consequences have on our children, both positive and negative, to see if they are achieving what we want to accomplish.

The issue of consequences is another place we are tempted to look for a one-size-fits-all approach. There are many good resources to help parents figure out consequences but, again, we are called to think wisely about our own children as we do this.

One of the principles we try to teach our children is this: Good choices have good consequences, bad choices have bad consequences. A decision to pick up their room may result in a reward, a compliment, an organized area where they can find what they're looking for, or simply a good feeling of accomplishment. A decision not to clean their room could result in a bad consequence like receiving discipline, constantly losing things in piles of laundry, and feeling disorganized in their own room. Consequences aren't necessarily about rewards and punishment. This teaches kids that every decision they make impacts themselves and others, and major and minor decisions alike always have some type of outcome. Natural consequences help place personal responsibility on the child. Whenever we can connect a consequence to a child's choice, we are teaching an important life lesson that they reap what they sow, positively or negatively.

We don't want consequences or discipline to feel random to our children. It is always wise to consider whether your choice of consequence is beneficial or detrimental. Kids should be able to connect the dots between choices and consequences and see the implications. When they cannot, it is our job to help them understand. They will not always agree with our consequences, but they should always be able to recognize why we have dispensed them.

Here's an example of what we tried in our home. When our children were young, we struggled to define the line between what I would call the minor offenses and the major ones.

Minor offenses in my mind were things that required obedience and self-discipline but did not rise to the level of moral failure—things like brushing your teeth, putting your shoes on, not talking with food in your mouth, remembering to put your homework in your backpack, etc. These were things we were talking about with our kids *ad nauseum*. Rather than nagging, threatening, or raising our voices in frustration, we looked for an immediate consequence that would reinforce the need to listen or obey the first time.

We wanted the consequence to be small enough so that if we had to impose it numerous times (which we would and did), it would not add up to weeks of grounding. It also had to be big enough that the kids felt its impact each time they ignored the rule. For example, we began telling our kids that every time we had to tell them to brush their teeth or put away their shoes (whatever the task might be), we would send them to bed fifteen minutes early. We knew that we might have to remind them three times to brush their teeth in the morning, and each time they would be told, "fifteen minutes earlier to bed." The cumulative effect was forty-five minutes earlier to bed, which did not strike them as too severe, yet also demonstrated the immediacy of consequences should they ignore doing the right thing. What we hoped to develop was self-discipline and good habits. We cared about obedience to our requests, but we tried to show patience by making the consequence more about teaching them something valuable.

Major offenses were things that were morally wrong, that caused harm or potential harm to self or others. This included things like lying, stealing, hurting your sibling, cheating on a test—things that had greater repercussions for their lives and character. These required more serious consequences, which included losing privileges, missing a major event, being grounded, etc. These offenses rose to the level of great concern, so the consequence was intended to demonstrate the gravity of their choices.

When we decide on a consequence, we usually stick with it because our goal is not to change a child's behavior in the moment, but to build character over a long period of time. Character is the sum of lots of interactions between parents and children and, of course, the work of the Holy Spirit. Being faithful as a parent includes teaching your child to obey because it is right.

Positive, proactive discipline is essential to helping kids grow. It may also be a way they see their need for Christ. God is a gracious, compassionate God. He is quick to forgive and assures us that he will empower us to follow his ways:

> "I will sprinkle clean water on you, and you shall be clean from all your uncleannesses, and from all your idols I will cleanse you. And I will give you a new heart, and a new spirit I will put within you. And I will remove the heart of stone from your flesh and give you a heart of flesh. And I will put my Spirit within you." (Ezekiel 36:25–27)

When Kids Say "It's Not Fair"

If you have raised children, you have heard these words.

"Why does Kim get to have a cell phone at twelve and I don't?!"

"Why does Kyle get to go to the movies with his friends and I can't?"

Our children view fairness as equality—same privileges, same blessings, same consequences, same responsibilities. And we as parents can sometimes confuse justice (what is right) with fairness (what is equal). We are called to love justice and to treat others without partiality (or favoritism). But does that mean that our parenting of each child must look and sound exactly the same?

Our children would love to turn that into a principle of equality in all things. However, that should not be the case. Again, wisdom and faithful parenting require us to know our children individually. This means we need to decide what responsibilities or freedoms each child is capable of managing. Would the freedom given to one be a blessing or stumbling block to another? The consequence given one sibling might be overwhelming to him, while another would be blasé and unmoved. Love speaks personally and with tenderness to each individual. It measures what they need and seeks to instill it in ways that attract them to what is good.

When we seek to be an expert at knowing each child, we begin to understand what consequences, rules, and boundary lines are needed to keep each one safe. Most of our rules and consequences will be similar for everyone in the home, but some will vary according to the maturity and needs of our children.

It can be very helpful to explain your thought processes to your children. Though they might not agree with you, when they see that you seek to be fair and have a rationale for what you do, they often learn to accept what seems unbalanced to them. It will sometimes seem "unfair," but the goal is to be wise and just.

Be careful not to judge the effectiveness of your discipline by your child's response. Our children are moral responders; they will choose whether they will become wise and learn from discipline, or whether they will be foolish and hardened in their response. They will choose whom they will serve. Instead, wrestle with these questions: Is my parenting loving? Is it consistent? Is it wise?

Meeting those standards will be challenging enough. You will fail, be convicted, and need forgiveness on those fronts alone. The rest must be left to the work of the Spirit in a child's life.

The Work of the Spirit

We've seen that we often fail to ask the Spirit to intercede in our children's lives. Perhaps the thought terrifies you. God's agenda for change rarely maps onto our own. You may fear what it might take to capture their hearts, or how far they will go with their poor choices and what the lasting repercussions may be. We can't know the answers to these questions. We can only parent in faith, plant the seeds, and entrust the result to God. It requires us to let go of the outcome, let go of control, let go of our agenda and reputation, our fears and insecurities. We lay down our agenda, knowing that there is One who is more committed to our child's welfare than we ever could be. We open our hands and say to the Lord, "My child is yours."

There is something incredibly freeing about handing our children over to the Lord. Though we are not able to produce change, God can do abundantly beyond all we could imagine. *He* can reach places inside our children's hearts and minds that no one else can go. He can and does perform miracles. It gives great hope to know that while I am out of options and resources, God never is.

It is usually not that we expect too much from God in these moments. Often we expect too little. He is the God who moves mountains, parts seas, raises the dead to life, and causes the blind to see. Is it really that we are demanding too much from God regarding our family, or is it that we are refusing to give over control? We have a loving Father who will show us the way when it feels hopeless and we feel helpless.

Any compassionate mother or father feels the sting of potential long-term repercussions for their children. Many times we are tempted to rescue our children from their poor choices when allowing them to fail and learn could have tremendous lifesaving power. When children are younger, the impact of our rescue is minor and easy to bounce back from. But as a child develops, the stakes get higher and the impact is sometimes ongoing and irreversible. Don't rescue your child from hard work, painful situations, or disappointment. Stand by them, walk alongside, shepherd and guide them, but do not spare them from important lessons. Teach them to surrender themselves to a loving Father.

You will have less apprehension over the opinions of others, more hope, and less despair when you commit your parenting to the Lord. When I entrust my children to God, their weaknesses, sins, poor choices, suffering, and even their rebellion will be used for good.

Psalm 16:6 says, "The *boundary lines* have fallen for me in pleasant places; surely I have a delightful inheritance" (NIV).

I like the image of boundary lines. One can look at boundaries as a hindrance that keeps me from doing what I really want—from being really happy or from _____ (whatever we desire in the moment). However, there is security within boundaries. Boundary lines are meant be both safe and pleasant. They are the guardrails that keep us safe on the highway.

Imagine driving down a mountain. On one side is a steep, hazardous cliff; on the other is the rocky mountain wall. Without guardrails, we could fall down the cliff on one side or crash into the mountain on the other. Without guardrails, danger is waiting. When life feels out of control, those guardrails are boundaries we come to value.

Do we help our children understand that the boundaries we put in place are meant as protection, not punishment? Do we help them see that God gives us guardrails so that life may go well for us? Do we help them see that God is not a killjoy whose rules are random, detached, and uncaring? Do we present ourselves this way when we erect boundaries, giving our kids reason to think that God is like that too?

So often our discussion of discipline revolves around defending the need for it, or defending the ways we implement it. Sometimes these arguments are necessary, but remember that Scripture emphasizes that the motivation for all discipline, rules, and consequences is *love and safety*. Not for primarily ourselves (though we reap the blessings as well), but for our child.

It is good counsel to stop focusing on behavioral change. Cease "trying" to make things turn out a particular way and just do the hard work of godly parenting. Let the Lord do the rest. As Galatians 6:9 says, "Let us not grow weary of doing good, for in due season we will reap, if we do not give up."

As the John Bunyan quote reminded us, if you don't delight in your children, you have no right to admonish them. Meaningful, loving relationships with our kids are the foundation for any discipline we impart. The success of remedial discipline is continually determined by the relationship you build in proactive training.

An Alternative to Micromanaging

Brittany is a responsible ninth grader. She gets good grades, keeps up with her work independently, and is fairly agreeable when asked to do tasks around the home. Although these things are true, her parents express concern. She is naïve about many things. She is guilelessly accepting of people and a lacks a healthy level of caution in relationships. She'd like to have a cellphone and is asking to join some of her friends on social media sites. She wants to begin working at an art center which offers many teen classes where she would meet new friends.

Parents often struggle with this reality: the older our kids get, the weightier their decisions become. There is a great deal we want to protect our children from. Given these facts, parents are often tempted to micromanage in an effort to prevent bad things from happening because of a child's poor decisions. Parents may have good intentions but can become overbearing when driven by fear. As a counselor, I want parents to focus on helping their children grow in independent decision-making. The goal is for children to have the godly character and appropriate knowledge to navigate all that they will encounter as they mature. Ultimately, we want children to have two things that go hand in hand:

- Good, wise discernment: the ability to know if what is going on at a particular moment is good or bad.
- Strong character: biblical convictions and integrity so that good decisions can be made joyfully, even when parents aren't present.

Good Discernment

We want our children to know whether something that is said or done is good or bad—whether it's in an email, on Facebook, Instagram, in a text message, at a sleepover, a party, or on the playground. Children tend to think in black-and-white terms, which makes it difficult for them to discern the gray areas of life. Often children associate "good" with people they like who are "nice," and "bad" with people they don't like who are unkind. As a result, it can be difficult for them to discern good from bad in someone's action and motivation. Children need to understand that it's not a matter of who said something (someone they like or don't like), but whether what was said or done is good or bad. "Is what this person is telling you right or wrong?" "Is what is happening right now good or bad?" "Does this build up or tear down?" These questions give our children a framework to judge actions, behavior, and speech—their own and others. By asking your children one of these questions, you teach them how to examine their behavior in light of what is good, right, and loving. Such questions also teach them to be more aware of the ways peers and adults might be influencing their decision-making. We want kids to evaluate the words and actions even of trusted adults. This ability will help them to decide whether it is wise to keep company with certain people.

As children learn discernment, there will be times when they will have to say "no" to their own desires and to others. It can be difficult for adults to say no, so must we expect that it will be even more difficult for children to do so. It puts them in social jeopardy and requires them to battle their own sinful desires. But the ability to say no and stand up for what is right can be strengthened through open, honest conversations, good role playing, and helping kids think outside the box. As you teach your children, ask the Lord to help you to be patient with their failures. Remember that you still fail in saying no at times. Our kids, too, will fail at times. We should expect that to happen. The goal isn't perfection. The goal is wise conversation that helps kids to know what to do when they encounter the gray areas of life.

Strong Character

When we arm our kids with a framework for discerning their experiences, we help orient their life as a life lived in God's world. That is, a life lived with God's purposes in view and under his command. Knowing that we live in God's world provides a sense of safety that our Father can be trusted and will give us the wisdom and clarity we need. His ways are truly better than our own. When we live life recognizing this, obedience becomes a delight. And as we practice obedience, we grow into the likeness and character of Christ. The stronger a child's character, the more discerning and cautious the child will be in situations that feel unclear.

As parents, we must cast this vision for our children and provide many opportunities to practice it, think about it, and live it out. When kids are equipped with this kind of worldview—that living life as God requires is good because he is good—we are inevitably going to see them grow in character and integrity through the power of the Spirit. The godly values and ethics that you develop in your children will then guide them as they make decisions. They will experience temptations and confusion at times—they may even dabble in something—but they will likely feel conviction and know that God offers a way of escape.

This approach is not about strong-arming our children into good character. Instead, it is about modeling a genuine love for the Lord and his ways. It is about a conscious effort to woo our children to Christ. This doesn't happen overnight. It requires a commitment to a worldview and lifestyle that can never start too early—and is never too late to begin.

Parenting Toolbox
Taking a Closer Look at Rules—for Both Parents and Children

- Distinguish between rules that are moral (those you teach to instill good character and godliness) and those that are about good skills and habits (those you teach to encourage good hygiene, organization, healthy eating habits). How do you talk about the differences in rationale to your children?
- How do your child's development and needs shape the rules or routines you put in place? Some rules might be for a season or a particular developmental stage in a child's life. (Some examples are rules about bedtime and morning or after-school routines.)
- Other rules may be needed longer due to a child's consistent weakness. (Some examples are monitoring good hygiene, requiring accountability with schoolwork and homework, and limiting technology use.)
- Can you articulate how the consequences for bad habits differ from the consequences for disobedience or sinful behavior? The two may sometimes be mingled together, but often we treat them equally in ways that are discouraging to our children. How does this occur in your home? What consequences help instill good practices in your home (loss of privileges, early bed times, redoing chores or homework, etc.)?
- What expectations do you have for your children's behavior and character? Do they exist because of your deep conviction that this is what God requires of your children, or are they based on ideas you value (strict routines vs. no routines, a quiet home vs. a chaotic home)? Not all of these preferences are bad. We all have subtle personal preferences that can shape our expectations for

our children, and they must be examined. Are your rules about an easier life for you as a person, or about a desire to help your family function well and to help your children mature in faith and character?

- Brainstorm with your children about the rules that operate in your home. List them together. You may be surprised at how many your children come up with. Ask them how they feel about the rules. Do they think they are fair? Talk with them about why they exist. Ask them if any are outdated or unhelpful and be willing to consider their input.

Reflection Questions

1. How did you experience family rules growing up? How has that shaped the way you've established rules? Does this chapter challenge you to think differently or does it affirm what you are doing?
2. How have you developed consequences for your children? Discuss their value in discipline. Have the consequences evolved over time? Why or why not?
3. How well have you explained the reasons for the rules in your home? Consider asking your kids what rules or consequences they disagree with and why. It will give you insight and provide an opportunity for further discussion.
4. How do you talk about fairness in your home?

CHAPTER 6

Building Bridges to Your Child

Nine-year-old Xavier is on Xbox Live every day. When he is not on the Xbox, he is on Instagram with his friends. After an hour of nudging and suggesting that he turn off social media, his mother forces him to get off the computer and begin his homework. Conflict ensues, with Xavier's constant backtalk amid a rush to complete the parental to-do list so that he can rejoin the social media world.

In situations like this, parents tend to look at technology as the problem. And I admit that technology can be a challenging issue. However, the real issue is that our children are learning to prefer their peers to anyone else. The reigning voices in their lives are those of their friends. This is hugely problematic. Technology has swung the door open wide to regular, uninterrupted access to that influence. Media, entertainment, and peer culture are actively striving to shape our children's values and ideas. With media/technology infiltrating our homes and saturating our children's lives, our kids are exposed to it almost every waking hour. As they age, they often begin looking to their friends as their source of knowledge and wisdom. Now the gate has opened wider, at earlier ages, to steer our children's hearts and minds toward their peers. We as parents must see the danger here and address it.

Peer Group Preference and Influence

As children develop, it is natural that they form bonds and relationships outside the home, and that such relationships have an influence on them. Rather than try to shelter our children from this, we should intentionally surround our kids with positive relationships worth emulating and enjoying. What is not natural or beneficial is that their source of modeling and wisdom for life is found horizontally, not vertically. It is from God that all wisdom flows on how to live a godly life. Parents and families are then intended to demonstrate that wisdom to our kids.

The most powerful influences are those we accept without question. Kids' attraction to their peer group is strong for many reasons: the desire to be accepted, to attract attention and affection, to gain power and be in control, etc. Whatever the reason, be aware of your child's susceptibility to looking for connection in the least healthy places.

If our relationship with our children is weak, it opens the door for another to come in and court them. Even when our bond is strong, children are still drawn to seek acceptance from their friends. We need to be right there in the mix with them, meeting their peers (and their families), influencing the role they play, the amount of time they share, and the quality of time they share.

When our kids are allowed to, they will look to their friends for the rules on how to dress, look, act, and talk. Their peers will tell them what to read, watch, and listen to, what to value, desire, disdain, or emulate. Many parents are dismayed by the choices their kids are making without recognizing the influences that got them there.

Am I overstating the issue? Am I worrying too much about the influence of friends when it has been happening for decades? What do children who are driven by peer preference expose themselves to? The influence of peers is not necessarily harmful nor abnormal, but the level of control and dominance is alarming.

When kids connect with unwise companions, they are giving themselves over to a precarious, immature hierarchy of power. This leads to many issues we now see in youth, including:

- A false sense of maturity and misplaced confidence (arrogance) in their self-knowledge
- An inability to occupy themselves or be alone
- Tolerance for bad behavior and inappropriate peer demands
- Intolerance of wisdom
- Mocking what is good or wholesome
- Turning a blind eye to immoral behavior
- Disparaging authority and adult values
- A lack of humility and teachability
- Glorifying crass, vulgar conversations
- Limited relationships with encouraging adults
- Idolizing/imitating peers
- Proneness to alienation and isolation
- Sexting and risky behaviors
- Degrading sexuality and sexually acting out
- The risk of becoming victims or bullies

Meaningful relationships speak to the conscience, providing a reference for what is good and right and how one should live. But typically, peers assume no responsibility, nor do they feel bad about their impact on your child. They can do significant damage. If peers replace parents, your children will carelessly follow the requests and demands of their friends. Parents face stiff competition from a culture that discourages parental bonding and encourages peer preference.

The Disintegration of Parental Authority

Ava was thirteen years old when her parents came to see me. For most of her upbringing, Ava had been eager to please,

101

happy-go-lucky, friendly, and close to her parents. Now she was argumentative and attached to her phone and social media. She fought over things like her clothing, lunch menu, and (especially) any and all technology restrictions. Ava's parents were surprised and frustrated by her sudden change. They found themselves resorting to punitive responses in the form of rebukes and threats. Ava in turn responded with anger and withdrawal, becoming more convinced that they were unreasonable and did not "get her." Ava was treating them like equals, as though they had no right or authority to speak into her life.

Ava's parents did not believe that yelling and threatening were helpful, but they often found themselves resorting to those responses to parent her. They were exhausted from handing out more and more consequences and punishments. They knew they had lost their God-given authority in her life.

Biblical parenting is the God-established, loving, judicious authority in the hands of parents. Parental authority is the responsibility to lead, oversee, and direct in a home, and to do so in a wise, godly manner. It is trustworthy, acting on behalf of those it governs, and doing what is right and just. It understands the need to direct, instruct, and establish rules in a benevolent manner. This authority is Christlike and points children to a God they can trust and follow.

> "Honor your father and mother, that your days may be long in the land that the LORD your God is giving you." (Exodus 20:12)

> Children, obey your parents in everything, for this pleases the Lord. (Colossians 3:20)

Often when children rebel, they are rejecting parental authority. At times this is due to defiance within the child. The influence of their peer group, as well as an open cultural aversion for authority, contribute. There are social values working against the relationship between a parent and child. In an attempt to reinstate our parental rights, we are sometimes tempted to take the above passages, read them to our kids, and demand that they comply. I don't find that most children bow their heads humbly and repent of their behavior when we respond this way. Rather, they react with a readiness to battle for control and independence.

I believe that much of the fault lies with us as parents. We have lost our influence on our children. We often unknowingly give up our authority or presume it is developmentally natural and appropriate to do so. And as adults, we have become preoccupied with our careers, work pressures, hectic lives and our own adult relationships, unwittingly modeling an undue dependence on peers.

Is it any wonder that kids look outside the home for someone or something to guide them (primarily their peers)? When much of our time is spent keeping our children busy rather than engaging them in relationship, they are bound to stop looking to parents as a voice or authority in their lives.

Children are engaged at school all day (with peers), then in sports (with peers), and in lessons, hobbies, and scheduled events (with peers) non-stop. When they are home, they are doing homework or chores, or occupied by the computer, internet, gaming, or play dates (all generally with peers). All this makes parents irrelevant for much of their daily experience.

Activities and busy schedules are not wrong, but we must be aware of how much time we are actively engaging our kids in meaningful relationship with us versus keeping them happily occupied. One fosters intimacy, the other fosters detachment. Do not be mistaken: kids do look for guidance and authority, and they will likely turn to the influence that has captured their admiration and trust. If we have been relationally absent, why would they accept our authority? In your child's experience, it has been detached and irrelevant. By the time we realize this has occurred, kids have committed themselves to their peer group as their trusted voice of authority.

Parental powerlessness is difficult to accept. It is tempting to minimize and excuse it. We chalk it up to "teenage attitude" or "kids these days . . ." We justify it as a natural independence; they are growing up and unsurprisingly distancing themselves from us. However, their need for emotional connection and meaningful support does not dissipate. Our role and influence change as our children grow, but we should not cease to have a voice and, more importantly, a relationship.

Perhaps we place the blame elsewhere, saying that it is the school's fault, their peers' destructive influence, or our child's rebellious spirit. We then look for ways to gain our authority back. Sometimes we resort to intimidation or consequences: we strong-arm them, demand, shame, or lecture them. Sometimes we try to buy their affection, attention, or compliance with material possessions, freedoms, or passivity in discipline. Many of us look for books, techniques, or tools that will offer a quick fix, a "magic bullet" that is guaranteed to work. We tend to see the problem as a badly behaved child rather than considering that it may be a relationship problem as well.

Parents need to fulfill the responsibilities that authority brings. We must earn our children's admiration and trust. We need to prioritize building strong, devoted relationships with them. The more godly authority we possess, the more those under us will desire to submit to it, because it will be founded on a trusting relationship. In it, we will have spent years displaying care for our children, sacrificial giving, genuine compassion, and being for them—an intimate knowing and being known by them.

Authority is not about force, power, or dominance. Power leads to temptation and potential abuse, used for our own benefit. We should never use our authority to inflict guilt or shame in order to gain compliance. When this happens, authority is self-seeking, corrupt, and anything but biblical. Parental authority is about Christlike leadership that seeks the good of those it leads.

Authority serves in many ways. Here are a few:

- It builds respect and cooperation.
- It creates an atmosphere of deference and admiration.
- It provides security and connection with children.
- It encourages a child's healthy dependence on parents for spiritual and emotional nurture.
- It models a reliance on wise counsel, especially from the Lord.
- It models a proper respect for leadership and governance.

As a counselor, I am trained to find ways to build trust and engage young people. I rely on techniques, skills, and tools for drawing them in and speaking into their world. However, all the skills and tools in the world cannot substitute for a trusting relationship. We as parents can spend far too much time reading about the latest parenting tricks and techniques, whether it is to get our kids to eat veggies, comply without complaining, or something else. None of this can take the place of a secure, loving parent-child bond.

Many parenting experts cringe at the idea that parental authority, rightly implemented, is a benefit to children. Instead, parental authority in the home has been replaced by professional advice on how to get kids to do what they should. When we think that those parenting methods are inadequate, we move to consequences, rewards, incentives, and behavioral charts. The real issue is that we have lost godly parental authority in our homes. It is painful but necessary to admit this if we are to turn the ship around. The most meaningful thing you can do for your children is show them love in a rightly ordered leadership.

In Ava's situation, her parents' God-given authority had been rejected and replaced with the opinions and attitude of her peers. Although it is hard to pin down where things went off the rails, it became important to get things back on track. It required Ava's parents to repent of all their harmful emotions and reactions and to believe that God had equipped them for the task. They had to ask the Lord to give them guidance and clarity as they responded to their daughter. They needed wisdom to know when to speak and when to listen, when to hold their ground despite her volatile reactions, and when to demonstrate grace and mercy.

Despite Ava's belief that her parents were inadequate and irrelevant, they chose to continue parenting her, cultivating relationship and extending an invitation to connect with them. They grieved, they fought frustration, and they prayed consistently for transformation in their daughter. Then they released her to the Lord and continued to try to steer Ava. Whether or not Ava ever exhibited change, they committed to asking the Lord what it looked like to love a child whose heart was hardened toward them.

The Answer: Building Relationship

Training and skills cannot replace natural God-given connection and affection for our children. We all have experienced moments with our children (I hope) where they warm our hearts and make us feel close with them; we experience their vulnerability and we instinctively feel protective. An embrace, a loving smile, and endearing words help bring out all that is good and parental in us to guard, shepherd, and care for them. Actions or words that show that they want to attach to us soften us and draw us near.

When we confront sinful behaviors, rejection of our authority, or indifference to our kindnesses, it is essential that we keep building bridges with our children. Sometimes it is difficult to like our kids, let alone love them. Children often have no idea how much pain they inflict or work they require, nor should we presume that they understand. It may seem like a hardship to move toward someone who is rejecting you or screaming in your face, but your willingness to do so will speak volumes.

A commitment to love without expecting any in return will enable us to keep building connection, risking rejection, and responding with grace. We need to continue to model a nurturing relationship even when our children do not reciprocate. That said, most kids long for closeness with their parents. No matter how hard it is now, or how long the relationship has been broken, you can rebuild those bridges.

Our children will only see us as role models if they have a loving, nourishing relationship with us and they have confidence in that relationship. Even as kids grow older, they still long for emotional closeness, perhaps more than physical affection. They wonder when Dad will get home and how to get in touch with Mom. They care about your opinions and your pride in something good they have done. Why? Because you have demonstrated that they matter to you even when you have not mattered to them. You know them and they cannot escape the security of knowing and being known by someone intimately.

When our kids long to be near us, learning and modeling can take place. Imagine the impact a meaningful connection with your children can have as you seek to connect them with the Lord. Do you make Christ look beautiful to your kids? Do you speak about Christ and emulate him in a way that makes your children want the same kind of relationship? Are they inspired to connect with their Creator?

When we don't demonstrate love to our kids, we lose the ability to draw them to Christ. We need to provide direction and guidance, to help them know what works and what doesn't, what is appropriate or inappropriate—to show them that they need wisdom outside themselves. Children are looking for direction; the question is, from whom? It does not matter how wise, clear, or forceful we are if we have not won their trust and respect. If we have not built a relationship with them, we will lose them. They will not want to follow us, and may reject following the Lord. We want him to be their compass and, for that to happen, they must connect to us, see him in us, and value our input.

Our kids are not looking for perfection, but love, compassion, and humility. It's our responsibility to consider our actions and to confess, repent, and reconcile with our kids when needed. In the absence of parental guidance, kids will find someone else, and it will almost always be their friends. An eagerness to comply, win approval, and gain acceptance can be very dangerous when children seek it from a peer group of immature, persuasive peers. That peer group will not be forgiving and gracious. They will give the impression of acceptance, but the strings attached will be huge.

No matter how well-meaning we are, we will lose our kids if we do not proactively work to build bridges with them, to maintain trust and close connection. It is difficult when you do not have children who are open to guidance; however, it is our responsibility to continue to fight for them, not against them.

A strong relational bond will not endure if we do not actively pursue our kids regularly and vigorously. This means we laugh with our children, we play with them, and look to affirm them and show that we like them. We demonstrate that we know them well and help them to know themselves. We point out their gifts and strengths, and the things we love seeing in their lives. And we gently, graciously show them their weaknesses, sins, and blind spots that they might see their need to depend on Christ. It is always our responsibility to build these bridges; we should never assume that it should fall on the child. They lack the position, the maturity, and the sense of purpose to do so.

How do you begin? I'll suggest a few ideas, but you must be an expert at knowing your own children and finding ways to connect. For one of our children, playing chess or a board game shows that I love him; for another child, that would be pure torture. For one of my daughters, it is letting her lay on our bed at night to chat about whatever is on her mind. For another child, it is not allowing him to hide, but working hard to draw out how he thinks about school and peers. I commend you to the task of getting to know your own family, applying wisdom, and pursuing them faithfully.

Parenting Tool Box
How to Build Relationship

1. Enter their world. Be "in their face" in a friendly, warm, non-obnoxious way.
2. Emphasize your interest in relationship over behavior. The time to address behavior will come, but you want your child to trust that you are for them.
3. Entice them to join you in relationship. Find ways to simply enjoy being with them with no set agenda. A walk, a card game, an ice cream or coffee run—all are ways to connect with them for no reason but to enjoy being with them.
4. Show genuine interest and delight in them with gestures, words, notes, and actions. Look for the small gestures, not only when you are pleased with them, but for seemingly no reason at all.
5. Establish routines of building closeness: reading together, walks, having meals and conversation, etc.
6. Commit to reconciling and reconnecting/building bridges when a rift, conflict, or argument occurs.

Reflection Questions

1. What relationships have you encouraged your children to foster outside your family? How would you evaluate the influence that these people have had on your children? Positive or negative?
2. Are there relationships you would choose to eliminate from your children's lives? Why do you allow those relationships to continue? Are there ways you can slowly move your children away from negative peer influences?
3. How do you define and understand parental authority? How does it compare with the way it is described in this chapter? How do the ideas put forth in this chapter differ

from your upbringing? Do they align with how you exercise authority in your home? Why or why not?

4. What can you do to increase, in loving, healthy ways, your parental influence on your children? Are there things you need to repent of to your family?

5. Brainstorm ways you can build bridges with your children. What does it look like to meet each child in meaningful ways? How are you doing this already? Where do you need to grow?

Part II

PARENTING BY FAITH APPLIED

CHAPTER 7

Parenting a Difficult Child

Do you have a child you find hard to parent? If so, have you wondered if the problem is your parenting? Have you struggled to stay positive and faithful with your child in the midst of the day-to-day battles? I have grappled with both. Here are a few brief reflections that have helped me to stay oriented to God as I parent.

Is It Me?

First, I begin with the question: Is it me? Is my parenting the problem? Some of the most burdensome moments for a parent are when it is clear to those around you that your child is defiant or difficult. When family problems are out in public, it might cause you to worry. What does this say about me as a parent? Am I doing something wrong? And what are other people thinking? Maybe they assume that your child's behavior is a result of inadequate parenting or something else amiss in your home. People may even be bold enough to share their views, without any sense of the shame they are heaping upon you. You feel marked, even judged, by your child's personal struggles. You hang your head around people who "know" about the problem. You assume that they see you as a failure and wonder if they are right. If you were a good parent, surely your children would be well-behaved, love God, and have good manners! After all, their children are not insubordinate.

If you feel defeated by your child's behavior, then you (and your critics!) have bought into the belief that good parents produce good children and bad parents produce bad children. This might seem downright biblical. If you raise a child in the way he should go, he won't depart from it, right? So it follows that if you were godly enough, wise enough, and patient enough, then your child would not be so rebellious.

It seems as if the right formula is: Love + Discipline + Godly instruction = Good kids.

And because, at times, this formula *does* seem to work, you determine that the problem must be in your parenting.

But this is a faulty, unbiblical approach. Good kids can come out of horrific family backgrounds, and rebellious, willful kids can come out of loving, Christian homes. Children are born with hearts that are wooed by their own desires and fears. They choose for themselves the type of person they will become. There is an active moral responder on the other end of your parenting—one who chooses whom he or she will serve. And there is no way a parent can ensure the outcome. The burden of thinking that you can might tempt you to give up or resort to poor or ungodly parenting (e.g., anger, yelling, harshness, despair, backing down, or backing away completely) because it might appear to work in the short run.

What then are you to do? Here are two recommendations:

1. **Evaluate your motivation.** Though you are not responsible for your child's bad choices, could it be that, without realizing it, you are adding to the problem? You can desire a good thing yet become driven by bad motives. If you are frustrated, despairing, or angry because of the challenges you face with your child, ask yourself: What agenda is dictating my parenting? Do I care too much about my own comfort or reputation? Do I desire a well-behaved child who causes me few problems or struggles? Do I want a child who makes me look good, who is productive, smart, and kind? Am I embittered because I have invested myself in this child and see no results? If you answer

yes to any of these questions, consider confessing the desires that grip your heart as idols, good desires that have become ultimate desires. Ask God to give you the grace, fortitude, and wisdom to parent your challenging child. Ask him to show you how to respond to your child out of love and concern for his or her well-being, not your own.

2. **Remind yourself of what God calls you to as a parent—** no more, no less. He calls you to love your children, to model a Christlike character and lifestyle, and to respond wisely and thoughtfully to their struggles. You are to encourage a personal relationship with the living God and, to the best of your ability, help them grow in the midst of their weaknesses, pointing them to Christ so that they can be conformed to his image. Though God expects you to parent with consistent love and wisdom, he does not hold you responsible for results that are driven by your child's sin or rebellion.

Stop trying to make things turn out a particular way and ask God to help you persevere in the hard work of godly parenting. Do not judge its effectiveness by your child's response. Simply wrestle with these questions:

- Is my parenting loving?
- Is it consistent?
- Is it wise?
- Is it fair and just?

Dedicate yourself to be what God requires of you and live it out fully before your child. Trust the Spirit to work in you and each member of your home. Persevere in your calling and watch the Lord work.

How Do I Stay Centered?

Still, the parenting challenges are likely to continue, which leads to the second question: How do you stay centered on God as you parent a child with ongoing behavior issues?

One of my children often finds herself in trouble. Early on, I became acutely aware of how often we were disciplining, addressing, and correcting her. Though her behavior very much needed correction, I found it discouraging. I felt strict and unyielding when I so desired to be encouraging and nurturing.

Every night I would spend a few minutes with her before bedtime. We would often talk about how the day had been. Over time, I found myself reflecting on Lamentations 3:22–23. It became a resting point for me as I interacted with her:

> The steadfast love of the LORD never ceases;
>> his mercies never come to an end;
> they are new every morning;
>> great is your faithfulness.

It encouraged me to remember that God's mercies are inexhaustible. No matter how much trouble my daughter had gotten herself into, or how upset we were over her behavior, God's faithfulness to our family would not waver. I would regularly try to end her day with this hope: "Honey, no matter what happened today, tomorrow is a new day. You are forgiven and loved. Tomorrow is a fresh start and God's mercies are new and waiting there for you."

My desire was to help her move from guilt or shame over her behavior to hope in One outside herself. I wanted to point her toward a good, loving God who offers himself to her in every circumstance. Little did I realize how the same sentences I spoke to her would be used over and over again—in my family, in my life, and in my counseling.

We all need the same hope that my daughter needs. We are so easily consumed by our circumstances and our failures. We need to be persuaded that what makes the difference is God-centeredness, a deep conviction that God is in the midst of our daily living. We must learn to trust not in the quality of our situation, but in the character of our Creator.

So here is my prayer for my daughter, for me, for my family, and for you, too:

Lord, remind me that my failure does not swallow me. When I wake up, your mercies will be there waiting for me. My circumstances will not overtake me, because tomorrow, or this afternoon, or in my next conversation, your mercies will be there—waiting. Your goodness, your grace, your faithfulness are new in every moment, in every circumstance. Help me to turn away from my laments and despair, and turn toward you in faith that your character is trustworthy. You are the God of steadfast love and great is your faithfulness to me. Amen.

If you are discouraged in your parenting, do not hang your head. Consider your heart, check your motives, and trust God with the results. His mercies for your child—*and for you*—are new every morning.

Reminders for the Discouraged Parent

1. When you can't figure out what to do, God will direct your path (Proverbs 3:5–6).
2. When you feel alone, remember that God does not leave you (Hebrews 13:5).
3. When you are exhausted from the fight, know that he will give you rest (Matthew 11:28–30).
4. When you feel you cannot cope, God says that he will supply all your needs (Philippians 4:19).
5. When it feels impossible, remember that nothing is impossible for the Lord (Matthew 19:26).
6. When you feel like giving up, know that his grace is sufficient (2 Corinthians 12:9).

7. When you cannot believe that anything good can come from it, know that he is able to do beyond all we can imagine (Ephesians 3:20; Romans 8:28).
8. When you are afraid of what's ahead, he is with you (Isaiah 41:10).
9. When you feel uncertain about what to do, he will give wisdom (James 1:5).

CHAPTER 8

Parenting an Anxious Child

Mason is a perceptive and emotional seven-year-old boy. He reads people well and has a particular awareness of danger and uncomfortable situations. Mason has heard clips on the news about a recent shooting. He asks his father if it is safe to go to school; he then asks his mother if he has to ride the bus. What if someone mean gets on the bus? What if someone has a gun? Despite their comforting words, he retorts, "But how do you *know* I'll be safe?"

Many families are seeing an increased anxiety enter their children's lives. With mass media and constant images, kids are subjected to the reality of global perils: things like war, ISIS, wildfires, internet hoaxes, and cyber-bullying. Kids are exposed more and more to things that might not touch their lives personally but reveal new, frightening possibilities. For kids with a disposition toward worry and anxiety, it can have a snowball effect.

Reasons for Anxiety

There are many reasons to be anxious, from terrorists to the flu, germs, dying, bugs, public restrooms, being bullied, making mistakes, getting bad grades, being laughed at, public speaking, not fitting in, losing a loved one—the list goes on. Some of the most common fears in young people today involve school performance, social acceptance (or the lack of), and the loss of a parent.

In Paul Foxman's book, *The Worried Child*,[1] he asserts that anxiety is the number one epidemic in the United States, and approximately 25 percent of the population struggles with it. Foxman describes how we often give children conflicting messages that the world is safe and unsafe. We walk into public schools with metal detectors and security guards. We talk about lining backpacks with protective metals. What message might that be giving to our children? We go through airports with multiple security checks, pat-downs, and bomb-sniffing dogs, yet we tell our kids not to worry.

Why do some children tend to struggle with anxiety more than others? There may be several factors. Every child is wired differently, with different strengths and weaknesses, and tendencies toward particular struggles or temptations. For some children, it is an innate temptation to fear. They are more alert to potential risk or tuned in to the peril others are experiencing. It creates in them a heightened sense of vulnerability.

Some kids have personalities that are more perfectionistic. They have difficulty relaxing, they like to please, are non-assertive, and tend to be conflict avoiders. Kids like this tend to struggle with the fear of man, the fear of disappointing or failing. They may place high expectations on themselves, leading to stress and anxiety. Another cause may be a prolonged exposure to stressful situations. Traumatic events, family turmoil, or an unpredictable lifestyle can lead to a sense of endangerment. The more we understand the cause of their anxiety, the greater success we will have in shepherding them through it, and the wiser and more practical we will be in speaking well into their experiences.

Chris is a sensitive, twelve-year-old boy from a loving family. He had very few intense experiences or losses until his grandmother passed away over the summer. Shortly after that, his grandfather also passed away, along with a family pet. Chris

1. Paul Foxman, *The Worried Child: Recognizing Anxiety in Children and Helping Them Heal* (Berkeley: Hunter House, 2004).

began worrying about his parents' well-being, though they were perfectly healthy. He became anxious about becoming ill or developing the flu. His parents became concerned when he refused to go to school one day because he knew several kids in his class had a virus. Chris's parents wondered if this was just a phase Chris was going through, a way of processing grief, or a developing struggle that needed intervention.

As a parent, how do we know when a child's fear is within a normal range, and when it is problematic and needs intervention? From a counseling standpoint, I would want to evaluate the degree to which it is impeding daily life. How frequent is the fear and anxiety? How intense is it? How long does it last? Is it preventing my child from engaging in daily activities? Does it keep them from taking healthy risks and engaging socially? In other words, is the fear controlling them or are they controlling the fear? Are they able to control/manage their anxiety, or does it control/manage them?

Children (adults too!) are tempted to find comfort by controlling or shrinking their world to what feels manageable. Some children look for security or comfort in routines, behaviors, objects, people, or the avoidance of certain things. The temptation for us as adults is to assure them that their fears are unfounded and bad things won't happen. Sometimes that is the case, but most of the time, I find that children are afraid of things that are real and possible. The truth is, they do live in a fallen, broken world where bad things happen. Cancer, danger, crime, and trauma are real. We fail and make mistakes; people make fun, bully, and say hurtful things. Life does not always turn out the way we would like it to. Will we be tempted to give our children false comfort or assurances we can't deliver? Or will we help them to navigate life in a precarious, broken world? Our hope is in the One who reigns over it all.

Parental Comfort vs. God's Comfort

When children are hurting, most parents would do anything to help bring relief. At times, this means that we might settle for solutions that provide short-term reprieves, but can cause secondary problems.

Take, for example, six-year-old Monica, who sincerely is afraid of the dark. Each night at bedtime, she begins her routine of checking under the bed and in the closet, turning on night-lights, and closing blinds. One night, she sees something disturbing on TV. Though you've gone through the nightly routine, she is still fearful. She looks panicked and is shedding tears, begging you to stay with her until she falls asleep. You've tried praying with her, playing soothing music, reading, a nightlight, and all the versions of comfort you can think of. It is getting late and you all are feeling sleep-deprived. Eventually you give in and allow Monica to settle into bed with you so that you all can get a decent night's sleep. But what starts out as survival tool for a rough season slowly becomes the new normal. Monica likes the warmth and closeness of her parents and resists the idea of returning to her room.

For other children, the appealing short-term solution is to distract them by allowing them to watch TV until they fall asleep. It is a solution for a difficult moment that we all might allow, a decision made out of exasperation. But those temporary solutions tend to quickly become permanent habits. Kids become dependent on the TV to fall asleep, or on having a parent in the room, or on sleeping in the parents' bed. It doesn't start out that way, but it becomes a benefit or reward for being afraid: "I get to stay up late, watch TV, sleep with my parents, or _____(fill in the blank) because I am afraid." Sometimes children might not want to get over their fears because it means losing something they have come to depend on or enjoy. What motivation is there to overcome fear if it means losing a special privilege?

If we are not thoughtful and careful on how we approach our children's fears, we may unwittingly give them reasons to maintain them!

In whatever comfort I provide my children, I hope ultimately to point them to Christ, who can meet them in the midst of their fear. As a parent, my comfort is limited; I cannot protect them from every fear. My comfort is flawed and prone to disappoint; I will fail them and be frustrated, forgetful, or sinful in my responses. And my comfort is not always accessible; I cannot go to school with them, live inside their heads, or be available every time they struggle. However, I can point them to the One who is always there, always available, whose comfort is perfect and limitless.

The Spirit can go places inside a child's heart and mind that we cannot. I am commissioned to image Christ in the comfort I provide my children, always leading them to Christ as their comfort. He can meet them in deeper and more meaningful ways than I as a parent can.

Second Corinthians 1:3–5 describes the comfort that we receive from Christ: "Who comforts us in all our affliction, so that we may be able to comfort those who are in any affliction, with the comfort with which we ourselves are comforted by God." We have a source for all we need to be for our children. We can provide comfort because it has first been given to us. We can offer hope because our hope was first found in him. As parents, we live out before our children what Christ is and does for us.

God's presence is always offered in the midst of fear. When we face tremendous fear and adversity, he offers us himself. We see this in Scripture over and over. Children need to find their hope and comfort there too. We don't want to guarantee that bad things won't happen, offer false hope, or make promises we can't possibly fulfill. Young people often see through this anyway, knowing that their parents can't promise that bad things won't happen. We want to point them to the One who can meet them in the midst of their struggles and fears. Some kids need short-term help (greater access to a parent, accommodation on the bus or in school, contact with a guidance counselor); some benefit from counseling or other, more intensive intervention. They all need to know that there is a God who walks with them through their fears. Parental wisdom is knowing—through prayer, thoughtful reflection, and wise counsel—what type of intervention their children need, while wisely and consistently pointing them to greater faith.

Giving Hope: What Message Do They Hear?

There are many shows and mini-series out today that entice young people with darker themes that portray life as meaningless. If you watch them, you will be struck by the very adult themes that are projected as the norm in high school life: partying, liberal sexuality, rape, drug use, foul language, violence against women, sinister secrets, and adults who are clueless about what is happening. These themes pervade many of the teen dramas that exist out there: licentiousness, do what feels good, look out for number one, and indulge in recreational sex and drug use, with little redemptive guidance. Adults are portrayed as the incompetent, ill-informed people who get in the way of what teenage reason knows to be the better way.

Kids need to know the reasons why God is relevant to them. They need to find meaning and identity in things that genuinely fulfill. They need hope.

Have we given our kids reasons why life is worth living? Have we fostered conversations about hard topics and convinced them that no topic is too hard for us to hear, no issue is off-limits, and we can handle even the most intimate details of their lives with genuine love and concern? We must be proactive in building connections with our young people. We must work tirelessly to engage them, proving our value in their lives when they are tempted to believe that what we have to offer is inconsequential or inadequate. Demonstrate that you are willing to go beyond the mundane, day-to-day, routine conversation. Talk about sexuality, abuse, pornography, sexting, suicide, peer pressure, loss, rejection, etc. Show them that you not only understand, but you have insight and perspective to offer that encourages and equips them.

In our home, we work hard to bring up the uncomfortable topics in order to make them easy and natural for our kids to talk about. It is our responsibility (and privilege) to model that it is safe to discuss these things as a family, that such dialogues are normal and good. We want our kids to know that we not only know these things exist, we have some empathy and insight to offer. More importantly, we want them to know that God speaks personally and meaningfully into their experiences. It would be common to find us sitting around the dining room table with six young people (widely varying in ages) talking about why kids (and adults) struggle with pornography or addictions, technology, or their cell phones. We ask our kids if any of their friends have made them feel rejected, or pressured them to do something that pricked their conscience. We talk about temptation, fear of man, and ways we might experience it as adults.

Let your teens know that they are not alone. Pursue meaningful conversation with your children. Be proactive in addressing hard topics before the issues enter their world. Be a redemptive guide speaking into the corruption they will be forced to wade through. Let them know there is One who fights on their behalf.

Thirteen Ways You Can Give Kids Comfort

1. **You are not alone.** "Even though I walk through the valley of the shadow of death, I will fear no evil, for you are with me; your rod and your staff, they comfort me." (Psalm 23:4)

2. **You have value.** "But you are a chosen race, a royal priesthood, a holy nation, a people for his own possession, that you may proclaim the excellencies of him who called you out of darkness into his marvelous light." (1 Peter 2:9)

"So don't be afraid; you are worth more than many sparrows." (Matthew 10:31 NIV)

3. **God sees your tears.** "He will wipe away every tear from their eyes, and death shall be no more, neither shall there be mourning, nor crying, nor pain anymore, for the former things have passed away." (Revelation 21:4)

4. **There is help.** "God is our refuge and strength, a very present help in trouble." (Psalm 46:1)

"For we do not have a high priest who is unable to sympathize with our weaknesses, but one who in every respect has been tempted as we are, yet without sin. Let us then with confidence draw near to the throne of grace, that we may receive mercy and find grace to help in time of need." (Hebrews 4:15–16)

5. **Your life has purpose.** "For I know the plans I have for you, declares the LORD, plans for welfare and not for evil, to give you a future and a hope." (Jeremiah 29:11)

6. **What you are going through is temporary.** "So we do not lose heart. Though our outer self is wasting away, our inner self is being renewed day by day. For this light momentary affliction is preparing for us an eternal weight of glory beyond all comparison, as we look not to the things that are seen but to the things that are unseen. For the things that are seen are transient, but the things that are unseen are eternal." (2 Corinthians 4:16–18)

7. **There is a way out.** "No temptation has overtaken you that is not common to man. God is faithful, and he will not let you be tempted beyond your ability, but with the temptation he will also provide the way of escape, that you may be able to endure it." (1 Corinthians 10:13)

8. **You are more than your outward appearance.** "The LORD sees not as man sees: man looks on the outward appearance, but the LORD looks on the heart." (1 Samuel 16:7)

9. **You cannot imagine what good lies in store for you.** "No eye has seen, nor ear heard, nor the heart of man imagined, what God has prepared for those who love him." (1 Corinthians 2:9)

10. **You will not always feel this way.** "We are afflicted in every way, but not crushed; perplexed, but not driven to despair; persecuted, but not forsaken; struck down, but not destroyed." (2 Corinthians 4:8–9)

"For his anger is but for a moment, and his favor is for a lifetime; Weeping may tarry for the night, but joy comes with the morning." (Psalm 30:5)

11. **You are greatly loved.** "I have loved you with an everlasting love; therefore I have continued my faithfulness to you." (Jeremiah 31:3)

". . . to comprehend . . . what is the breadth and length and height and depth, and to know the love of Christ." (Ephesians 3:18)

12. **You will not be put to shame.** "Fear not, for you will not be ashamed; be not confounded, for you will not be disgraced; for you will forget the shame of your youth, and the reproach of your widowhood you will remember no more." (Isaiah 54:4)

"Keep your life free from the love of money, and be content with what you have, for he has said, 'I will never leave you nor forsake you.' So we can confidently say: 'The Lord is my helper; I will not fear; what can man do to me?'" (Hebrews 13:5–6)

13. **God is up to good in your life.** "You meant evil against me, but God meant it for good, to bring it about that many people should be kept alive as they are today." (Genesis 50:20)

"And we know that for those who love God all things work together for good, for those who are called according to his purpose."(Romans 8:28)

CHAPTER 9

Parenting a Child with Disabilities

In 2013, my son Andrew was diagnosed with a degenerative disease that is gradually causing him to lose his vision. When the diagnosis came, it hit us like a ton of bricks. I felt sick to my stomach as hundreds of implications for his life began to sink in. What dreams would he no longer be able to fulfill? He wanted to be a baseball player or maybe an astronaut. Such things were no longer possible. He wouldn't be able to ride a bike, learn to drive, or likely live on his own. What would his future be like? Then there were the hundreds of implications for us as parents and as a family. I was not prepared. "Lord," I prayed, "I am not equipped to parent a child with this disease. I am the wrong person. I lack the knowledge, skills, and resources to help him. Lord, you've given this child the wrong parents. We are incompetent."

Unable but Equipped

We were baptized into learning what it meant to be parents of a child with a long-term disability. We were forced to go down a road we did not want to travel and we felt ill-prepared. I was now a member of a club that no one wants to join. I didn't want this for my child, and I did not want this for me. I repeatedly asked myself, "How could I ever be what he needs?" I am not being humble when I say that I am the worst person God could have picked for this task. Days will need to be spent in hospitals for tests, and I am someone who faints at the sight of blood. My family jokes that they simply need to start talking about injuries to get me to leave the room. How could I handle sitting in medical facilities?

I am also not an assertive person. Parents of special-needs kids have to be their child's advocate, to be uncomfortably assertive and tenacious. I was not up for the task. We are a large family with two working parents and limited time, energy, and resources. How and why would God think this was a good idea? There are so many others who are more competent to manage this than me.

And then, how could I tell him? How would I explain to my son that he has a condition that will take his vision away? I was afraid that he would question God and his goodness, and that he might become bitter and angry. I worried that the innocence of his trust in God would be corrupted by his suffering.

What I needed to be reminded of is that when God calls us to do something, he also equips us for it. I watched events unfold that demonstrated that he was already at work; he knew exactly what he was doing when he allowed Andrew to face this affliction. As we began adjusting to the diagnosis and pursuing resources for Andrew, we saw that the way God uniquely wired him was a resource in itself. Andrew is logical and gifted at figuring things out. For a visually impaired individual, using adaptive technology is a lifeline to communicating with others and becoming self-sufficient. Andrew has a natural propensity for it and took to it easily. Educational facilities and teaching hospitals would smile when he came in because he was so much fun to work with. He often showed them how to operate equipment when they forgot! They would brag about how well he was doing, and I watched him beam with pride.

But it all culminated for me on a Sunday afternoon when Andrew was recounting what was taught in Sunday school that morning. They had discussed the passage in John 9 where the disciples asked Jesus why the blind man had been born blind. I cringed as he began talking, wondering how it was handled (many did not yet know of his condition). When he finished talking about the lesson, I asked, "So, what do you take away from the story?" He replied, "Well, I learned that God can take even my disability and use it for good, for his glory. God doesn't waste anything."

God Wastes Nothing

It brought tears to my eyes. I had not yet used the word *disability* with him. I had not yet figured out how to help him grasp a good God while experiencing a crippling disease. While I struggled to know how I would speak to my son, God was already doing so and using my son to speak back to me! Andrew was modeling to me that God sees. God is not silent, distant, or uninvolved. He was already working, showing me the benefits of how he wired this boy, and using medical staff, Sunday school teachers, and others to demonstrate that he was present and very engaged.

God knew. He knew that Andrew's intellect and natural aptitude with technology equipped him for the challenges he would face with this disability. God sees. He knew that Andrew's positive outlook and natural curiosity would help him to use equipment and learn to read braille. God had prepared Andrew for such a time as this.

But then there was still me. Not only did I feel ill-equipped, but my thoughts still hovered around the loss I felt. As parents, we want the best for our children. We want to see them thrive and succeed and be all that they can be. I grieved, fearing that this might not be the case for Andrew. And I grieved for all the ways it would impact me and my parenting. I was discouraged by what I would have to learn and the ways in which my life would have to change. It brought out all of my insecurities and weaknesses. I feared that I could not serve Andrew in the way he would need to be served.

At some point, I was reminded of this verse: "My grace is sufficient for you, for my power is made perfect in weakness" (2 Corinthians 12:9). So I prayed. My prayer went something like this: "I will boast in my weakness that the power of Christ may be perfected in my life, my parenting, and my son. Though I do not want this for my child, for myself, or for our family, Lord, let your power shine through our brokenness and vulnerabilities." I prayed and prayed—and I began to see God work.

God knew. He knew that he would be stretching me and calling me to trust in ways where I struggled. He knew it would challenge me to be more assertive. He knew it would shake my confidence, but he wanted to show me that I can rest in trusting that he is good and will provide. God is up to something good in my life, though it is very challenging. He is also up to something good in Andrew's life. He will continue to use Andrew and who he is—all for his glory.

Strength in Brokenness

Once again God has shown me how he sees brokenness. He is not put off by it. Instead he uses it to reveal himself to us and draw us closer to him. We do not face the future alone. Our response is to trust him, even when we cannot see.

As the years have passed, Andrew's vision has decreased. He's hit middle school and he is facing new challenges both in his social life and his personal life. At times, he questions why God is allowing this. He has even felt somewhat angry at God for his struggle. We've walked alongside of him in times of great faith and in times of doubt. At new stages developmentally, he has to wrestle with new issues and questions. He will have to grapple with whether he can live independently and how he will learn to do so. He will have to wrestle with what dating and marriage might entail and if he could pass on this disease to his children. There will be times when people will judge him and limit him.

As parents, we never want to minimize the suffering in Andrew's life or offer simple, cliché answers. We know that God doesn't promise to answer our why questions, but he does ask us to trust him even when we do not understand. That kind of faith is hard for most adults, yet now, as a young teen, Andrew is being challenged to trust in this way.

Parenting a child with special needs requires a long-suffering perseverance with the unique needs and challenges your child faces. No one understands this better than another parent who has walked down this path. The particulars vary from disability to disability, and the implications vary from family to family, but the struggles are often similar.

When a family includes a child with a disability or special need, the entire family is impacted. Every family member is touched by it, to varying degrees. They are challenged to step up and help, learn more empathy, or advocate and stand up for their sibling. Intentional parenting does not simply mean helping the child with the disability; it also involves shaping the way the entire family understands the disability and engages with it. It means shaping their understanding of suffering and brokenness and why God allows them. It requires giving them the words to voice their questions and confusion and directing them to a God who meets them and answers personally.

CHAPTER 10

When Your Child Says,
"I Don't Know"

The book of Proverbs reminds us that we are to disciple our children (Proverbs 1:8). But to be good disciplers, we need relationships with our kids that are honest and open. We need to know what is really going on with them so that we can encourage godly thinking. It is our job to foster conversation in ways that draw our children out and give them reason to share their thoughts and feelings. Ask young people their opinion about topics. Demonstrate patience and interest in what they have to say. Ask young people what kids in their class, neighborhood, or youth group are talking about, struggling with, or driven by. My husband and I have found that in areas where our kids are hesitant to open up and share their own struggles, they will freely share about their peers' battles. In so doing, they give us insight into their lives as well. Kids will often open up about what their peers are doing when they are unwilling to talk about themselves. Look for the open doors into their lives that help you to understand what they wrestle with.

Kids don't always cooperate, of course. Sometimes they don't want to talk with us and, at a surprisingly young age, children learn that they can avoid engaging in thoughtful discussion by giving the notorious "I don't know" response to our questions. It can be maddening as a parent, and we are quick to resort to lecturing our son or daughter in those moments.

It Happens at School

When a student is not paying attention or doesn't have an immediate answer and says, "I don't know," the focus quickly moves to the next student. At times, the teacher answers the question for them. They've been let off the hook. A simple "I don't know" may prove slightly embarrassing in the moment, but swiftly dissolves into relief when the spotlight moves to someone else. The child can go back to mentally checking out, texting on the phone, or doodling in their notebook. One of our children mastered the skill of looking attentive while his mind was planning his next move on the Xbox. If he was asked a question, "I don't know" promptly moved the attention away from him and he could return to his fantasy world.

Sometimes this response is driven by fear: fear of giving the wrong answer, of being laughed at or publicly mocked. It might even be fear that they will get it right and be asked a follow-up question! Whatever the reason, kids learn that "I don't know" works when adults do not take the time to draw the child out in helpful, positive ways.

It Happens at Home

"Why did you cheat on that test? Why didn't you clean your room when I asked? Why did you lie about that?" When given the "I don't know" response, parents often lapse into lecture mode. We unleash our frustrations and a litany of reasons why what the child did was wrong. Meanwhile, the child checks out emotionally, endures the torment, and is never encouraged to understand what led to the poor choice. Very often, "I don't know" means that our children can avoid evaluating their actions or the heart motivations behind them.

133

It Happens in Counseling

Kids say "I don't know" instinctively, almost without thought. It comes with an expectation that I, as the counselor, will move to another topic, or do as many other adults do and answer the question myself. Perhaps I will begin lecturing as well, which simply requires the child to endure my rant. Do you see a theme here?

In all of these situations, children learn that this response keeps them from having to do the hard work of critical thinking or personal self-reflection. They may even avoid accountability, honesty, and vulnerability.

But letting children get away with such shallow responses does not help them, nor is it good discipleship. We need to find ways to get past such responses and help them gain insight into their own hearts. Proverbs 20:5 says, "The purpose in a man's heart is like deep water, but a man of understanding will draw it out." The question is, how can we draw them out? Biblical wisdom, knowing the child, and a deep commitment to listen are all indispensable.

Years ago, I attended a training session where I heard the results of research done with youth on the "I don't know" response. When asked the follow-up question, "Well, if you *did* know, what would your answer be?" kids gave a more responsive answer fifty percent of the time. Brilliant, isn't it? It confirmed what I'd already suspected. If I demonstrate genuine care, slow the moment down, and give kids an opportunity to really consider the question, they will often respond more thoughtfully. The follow-up question is not a magic bullet, but the principle behind it is. You are not taking no for answer. You are demonstrating that you want to hear and you will be patient enough to wait.

Here are some specific methods I use to handle the "I don't know" response.

- **Brainstorm with the child.** Sometimes a child may not know how to answer your question. They might also be afraid that they need to get the correct answer, so they freeze in uncertainty. At these times, it is helpful to brainstorm with the child about what might be going on. By offering them possibilities, I'm encouraging thoughtful interaction. I'm also *not* letting the child off the hook. Loving well sometimes means coming alongside someone to aid in greater self-awareness. After hearing several options, a child will often say, "Yeah, I think that's it." When this happens, it is often because I was able to put into words what they were thinking or feeling but were unable to articulate. At other times, they won't initially voice what they think for fear of admitting what they know to be true or shameful. By offering a possibility and modeling it as an option that does not shock me, it frees them to acknowledge it openly. Brainstorming with them also acknowledges that they could be motivated by multiple desires, thoughts, or reasons.

- **Wait them out.** For those who are simply unwilling, defiant, or lazy in their response, I have multiple goals. I want the youth to know that I care too much to accept "I don't know." What a child thinks matters to me and I genuinely want to understand, so "I don't know" can't be accepted as a final answer. I respond with, "Take a minute and think about it. I am willing to wait." Then I wait silently. The pressure is on. They stare at me; I stare at them. I am open and encouraging but allow for the uncomfortable silence. Silence can be a powerful motivator for those who are uncomfortable with it. I use it to my advantage—a type of positive pressure for kids to engage. More than that, I hope it truly demonstrates that they are worth waiting for. I will often encourage them by saying, "What you think and feel is important and I care. I'm in no hurry."

135

By showing them that they can't get out of the conversation until they engage, I hope they see me as a person who genuinely cares to know them more deeply. I don't need to move on to the next topic, nor will I be put off. It may be one of the few times someone in their world slows down enough to really wait and listen. It will not be lost on them.

There will be times when a child or teen digs in his heels and decides to go toe-to-toe with you, refusing to talk or open up. In those moments I try to make sure that I have not made the conversation into a battlefield. Rather, be willing to give them time, demonstrate kindness and patience, and affirm the relationship.

- **Gently encourage self-awareness.** As in my first example, I work to teach the skill of self-reflection. Once they start to talk, I urge them to consider their motives for what they said or did, and I gently challenge their responses to stimulate critical thinking and greater self-awareness. You can probe, offer alternatives or options, and notice what you've seen in other people. This helps children to know that there is no temptation that is not common to man. It demonstrates that we are not shocked or put off by what they are thinking. If we want to raise godly children, these skills are essential.
- **Be patient.** As adults, parents, teachers, leaders, and counselors, we can become much more winsome and patient when asking kids questions, especially in response to "I don't know." Do the hard work of drawing kids out. There may be times when you allow them to walk away from the conversation to think about things, but if you do, give a time frame to resume the conversation to show that the discussion is not over. Then follow up with them. Many a parent says, "This conversation isn't over!" What they really mean (or what the child hears) is, "I'll be watching you—or waiting to see what you do next." It is far better for your children to hear that they

are loved, that what they think is valued, and that their parents will continue to pursue them.

They may challenge you, reject you, or be angered by your attempts, but you will model care by your persistence. We do not always get to see the ways in which it helps them recognize our love for them, but Galatians 6:9 encourages us, "Let us not grow weary of doing good, for in due season we will reap, if we do not give up."

CHAPTER 11

When Your Child Says, "I Am Bored"

We have a frequent crisis in our home. It is the calamity of boredom. Our children might even consider it a catastrophe. "I'm bored" is repeated so often that it would not be an overstatement to say that these words echo continuously throughout our home, especially during any break from school. Holidays, summers, even Saturday mornings can be filled with boredom statements. These are children with limited media time but still in possession of Wii and Xbox systems, a pool outside their door, multiple games, toys, and other planned activities. Yet "I'm bored" rolls off our children's tongues with great frequency and personal displeasure.

As a result, Greg and I came up with a clever solution. We told our children that every time we heard the words, "I'm bored" (and all versions of boredom: "I'm tired," "Nothing to do," etc.), we would assign a chore. It might be to clean their room, sweep the porch, take the dog for a walk—something to occupy idle hands and encourage them to find healthy ways to occupy themselves. It didn't take long before the words slipped out of use and thereafter, my kids appeared to find ways to occupy their time. They played board games, went outside, played with one another, or read a book. However, though this is a clever solution (and a great way to get the house cleaned!), doing chores does not address their more fundamental struggles.

The Issue of Over-entertainment

First, young people struggle with being over-entertained. When left to their own devices, they will often turn first to media, which for the most part allows them to be passively entertained rather than actively engaged in a hobby or activity. By spending time on social media, video games, TV, or movies, they are quite literally entertaining themselves to mindlessness. Let me say that I am not anti-technology. I have a visually impaired son who will thrive in this world because he can use technology. It is his lifeline. There are technology apps and programs that are productive and educational for all of my kids. However, it only takes a little bit of research to uncover a great deal of documentation on the unfavorable effects of technology on young people. Doctors, educators, and developmental specialists are seeing the adverse side effects on children.

When there is a moment of silence or inactivity, the "adversity" of boredom descends upon them and they are used to having someone or something fill that void for them. They feel incapable of overcoming boredom on their own. Assigning a few chores makes that clearer, but it is only an external impetus for behavioral change. They need to learn to use free time more productively.

The Neglected Gift of Stillness

Second, we need to help our children develop the neglected gift of stillness. Something is lost when we don't know how to sit, be quiet, swing on a hammock, or take a walk without something bellowing in our ear. We all need to stop and smell the roses, experience creation, cease striving, and know that he is God. We need to learn to enjoy such moments as a delight, not a time of boredom. Like us, children need to learn to reflect,

139

contemplate, and meditate on the things of God. How will that happen if we do not try to instill this in our children?

Consider taking your kids out for a long hike or walk. You are getting them out in nature, spending time together, enjoying the fresh air, and physically wearing them out. I would challenge you even further to find ways to involve them in thought-provoking conversations. Get them talking about school, friends, their future goals, or anything that gives them a chance to open up, and you an opportunity to listen. This might feel like pulling teeth at first (or even longer), but it will be worthwhile. In our home, we joke that it is time for "forced family fun." The kids might complain at first, but they end up happy and content on the way home. It doesn't really matter what the activity is—a hike, bike ride, a coffee date, bowling—just something that encourages quality time together. Deuteronomy 6 talks about discipling our kids throughout the day. We must find ways to do so as we walk alongside them, live life with them, help with homework, or sit with them over dinner.

The Opportunity to Serve

Third, kids need to be less consumed by their personal comforts and desires and learn to think outside themselves. There is a world of service, job opportunities, education, and life to be lived out there, and they need to be nudged (or sometimes dragged) in the right direction. Teens are not going to wake up one morning feeling charitable and asking to serve in the local food pantry. We need to start early in their lives to cultivate generosity and a desire to serve. We want to instill in them a willingness to give of both their time and resources. As parents, we have to be willing to steer our kids toward service, imparting to them a desire to be other-centered. This will require us to give of ourselves.

The Problem of Idleness

Another way to understand boredom is through the lens of idleness. Many times one leads to the other or the two can be used interchangeably. Idleness is a term we often see in Scripture

(2 Thessalonians 3:11; Proverbs 31:27). It causes all kinds of trouble, especially with those who are busybodies and disruptive. It can lead to many other sins.

The state of idleness suggests that there is nothing valuable to merit our time or energy. However, as long as we have breath, we have something to do for the Lord. To combat the tendency to be idle, we should cultivate the habits of work, service, ministry, a healthy, godly enjoyment of pleasures and hobbies, and an enriching of our relationships. Even stillness is an active focus toward worship and meditation on the things of God.

There is always someone who needs help, prayer, or encouragement. We have unlimited ways to teach our kids to fill time with meaningful pleasure or work. When we see them struggling with boredom or idleness, we should look for ways to encourage them to think outside themselves, to work as unto the Lord, or to cultivate their gifts and interests.

Many Bible passages address idleness (Proverbs 19:15; 1 Thessalonians 5:14). Consider weaving them into your daily routine and conversations. Make it a priority to teach kids to find purpose and meaning in who God created them to be.

Here are some Scripture passages to consider as you disciple your kids through boredom or idleness:

1. Idleness stirs up trouble and leads to destitution (Proverbs 16:27–30).
2. Idleness leads to gossip and discord (1 Timothy 5:13).
3. Laziness corrupts a person (Proverbs 26:13–16).
4. Idleness leads to an undisciplined life or "mooching" off others (2 Thessalonians 3:7–9).
5. The diligent work hard and accomplish much (Proverbs 10:4).

The answer to boredom is not always work in the traditional sense. I don't want my kids to feel that work is all that they should value. Value can be found in significant relationships, in hobbies, in creation and beauty, and in many other experiences. Consider some practical ways that your family can:

- Serve others
- Volunteer for an organization
- Cultivate stillness and reflection
- Foster an appreciation for nature and creation
- Spend time with others in nursing homes, hospitals, or with shut-ins
- Enjoy hobbies and family projects
- Develop a love for reading
- Nurture one's natural gifts and talents

So, if your kids are bored at home, you might try the chore response. It does have a certain appeal! But recognize its limitations. It will not instill in them the godly character you really desire for your children. That only comes by carefully examining what captures their affections and equipping them to thoughtfully steward their free time.

CHAPTER 12

When Your Child Isn't Thankful

I am struck by how often I find that young people miss the experience of gratitude. Not a warm, fuzzy thank-you for a gift, but a deep, rich appreciation for life and what the person has been given.

What Gets in the Way of Gratitude?

1. **A society that cultivates discontent.** Mass media, advertising, and holiday seasons all cultivate a misconception of what we "need"; all encourage a hunger for more. There are literally thousands of images, commercials, and marketing ploys that are meant to create a sense of need. I "need" this new phone to be satisfied, this new product to be fulfilled. Advertising fosters a feeling of deficiency. It seeks to convince us that without the latest beauty product, invention, or gadget, we are lacking. They create a sense of inadequacy, and then offer the magic bullet that solves the problem. In Philippians 4:11–12, Paul rebuts this message: ". . . I have learned in whatever situation I am to be content. I know how to be brought low, and I know how to abound. In any and every circumstance, I have learned the secret of facing plenty and hunger, abundance and need."

2. **Entitlement** is the "belief that one is deserving of or entitled to certain privileges."[1] It tells me that I deserve that new iPhone or vacation, or peace and quiet when I come home after working a long, hard day. Entitlement then justifies whatever self-serving response that pours out of me when I don't get those things. Entitled desires quickly become demands that justify putting myself first and others last (if at all). But these things, no matter how much I desire them, are not innate human rights worth fighting for when I am deprived of them. They are simply wants that have risen to a level of necessity in my heart and mind. Genuine gratitude silences entitlement and reminds me that every good and perfect gift comes from above.

Ephesians 5:2 says, ". . . walk in love, as Christ loved us and gave himself up for us, a fragrant offering and sacrifice to God." Our goal is not to look for what we deserve, but to be poured out as an offering to others (Philippians 2:17). We are called to value relationship above material possession; ultimately, relationship with God, but also with one another. The more I teach my children to love God, enjoy each other, and serve others, the more they learn that it is better to give than to receive (Acts 20:35).

Entitlement and discontent are two attitudes that promote ingratitude, but there are ways to cultivate gratitude in your home. Here are some simple but practical ways to encourage this in your family:

- **Gain perspective on God's presence.** Life is about who God is, not what we own. His presence is the answer to every need, every fear, every suffering. Not because his presence removes the challenges of life, but because

---

1. *Merriam-Webster Dictionary*, accessed April 19, 2018, http://www.merriam-webster.com/entitlement.

it gives us perspective on the joy and power of knowing God personally. As your children watch you live life out before them—the way they see you talk about God, talk to God, and engage in life with God—this helps them to see that he is what satisfies.

- **Remember what God has done.** Instill in young people the ability to notice good things and to value them. Psalm 77:11 talks of remembering the deeds that God has done. So often in Scripture, we see this theme of remembering what God has done, not forgetting, calling to mind, and having hope. The practice of looking for and treasuring the good in everyday life deepens our pleasure in what we have. It reminds us that God is our provision and the source of all we need. That kind of gratitude is invaluable.

  Remembering can be done in many ways: with lists, journals, creative expressive exercises, memory boxes, gratitude jars, etc. Gratitude itself is not the end goal; we aspire for gratitude that points to the Lord, our Provider. He is enough. He is our source of contentment, pleasure, and satisfaction. All else is icing on the cake, blessings that flow from above.

- **Express your gratitude.** Express your gratitude to your own heart, to God, and to others. Write it down. The more we encourage kids to express appreciation and gratitude, the more it takes root. They benefit by voicing their thoughts, in seeing the pleasure they bring to others, and by living as an example to those around them. Encourage them to see good and to name it.

- **Serve others.** There is immense benefit to getting outside ourselves by focusing on the needs of others. We all need to see the world that needs our care. Caring well for others is deeply rewarding as we love others in ways that image Christ and make him known. There are endless ways to serve, using our gifts and our time to do babysitting, yard work, or preparing a meal for the disabled, elderly, disadvantaged, lonely, and homeless, not to mention the needs of churches, para-churches, and our own extended families. An awareness that others live with far less material possessions, and sometimes far more suffering, brings a truer perspective and a gratitude for what we have.

Gratitude moves us from a perspective of need to one of contentment. It acknowledges that no matter my condition, my possessions, my sufferings, or my blessings, they all point me back to the One who satisfies, in whom I am completely fulfilled.

CHAPTER 13

The Importance of Role Playing and Practice

As a parent, I want to create opportunities for meaningful and fruitful conversations with my children. I often use role playing as a means to accomplish that goal. In role playing, you present a situation to your children and ask them what they would do and say as they take on different roles in the story. For example, your child may not know what to do when a peer pressures him to lie or cheat. Role playing gives children a way to practice possible responses to such difficult situations. It allows them to think with you about situations they haven't encountered. This helps you understand how your child thinks by providing a window into his fears, his struggles with temptation, and the situations in which he might be caught off guard.

Learning to Apply Biblical Principles

Since kids tend to think in black-and-white terms, it can be challenging for them to wisely navigate the gray areas in life. Children may understand biblical principles but struggle to apply them in the moment. Role playing is an opportunity to take teachable principles—love, kindness, mercy, forgiveness, safety—and bring them into different situations. This type of conversation primes children to take one principle and apply it to a multitude of settings they might not have considered. It expands their understanding of the principle as they see it applied to different contexts, and it prepares them for many situations that may (or may not) happen. As you role-play, try for a range of possible scenarios, from the silly to the obvious, to the confusing, to the dangerous, to the impossible.

For example, your child could be an aggressor in one role-play situation and the pressured or attacked in another. Most children are not always the bully or always the sufferer. Develop a scenario in which your child is tempted to be an aggressor (maybe with a younger sibling) so that you can speak about love and patience. Then develop a scenario in which your child is the one being hurt so that you can talk about how to stay safe and how to forgive.

Fostering Open Communication

I have found that the more I am willing to talk about the many "What ifs" with children, the more they are willing to say, "I'm not sure. What do I do when that happens?" Role playing becomes an open door for discipleship. By asking your children questions that encourage them to think and make decisions, you help prevent them from being stuck in a situation where they don't know what to do. Inevitably our children will get stuck, but role playing and intentional conversation will decrease these occurrences.

As your children mature and learn, don't forget to encourage them! You don't always get it right and neither will your kids. It's important to tell children, "Do your best and we will be proud of you. And if you do get it wrong, we will talk about what happened." This assures children that they won't be punished for trying to apply what they've learned from you. Often refinement is what is needed, not punishment.

I encourage you to incorporate these conversations into normal, everyday life. Our van is one good place to get my kids talking about these "What ifs?" The car is an undistracted place for kids to reveal their thoughts and experiences, and the ride gives you time to help process and interpret those experiences. But anywhere you can get your kids to talk about different situations is a good place! My hope is that parents will be on the lookout for teachable moments and take on the responsibility of proactively creating opportunities for conversation through activities like role playing.

Practice Makes Permanent

You've heard the old adage, "Practice makes perfect." Recently my son came home from school and said, "Mom, do you know that practice really makes *permanent*?" He then proceeded to explain to me what his teacher had taught him: If you learn to do something the wrong way (and repeatedly do it the wrong way), you will learn permanent bad habits, which will likely result in bad outcomes.

I mulled over his statement and realized that this rang true in many areas of life. I decided to turn it into a teachable moment to talk to my kids about ways we do this in our spiritual lives, thought lives, and relationships.

What Are We Practicing at Home?

My fear is that as we teach our children various behaviors and habits, our focus is often about external behavior only. Our instruction centers on what to do and when to do it, without any real connection to why. Ultimately, everything our children do should stem from a love for God and others. ("I love my sister so I allow her to choose the movie," or "I love God so I pick up my room in gratitude for the belongings he has blessed me with.") We want to teach our children to do good things for godly reasons. This addresses the motives behind our behavior, as well as the attitude with which we do such tasks.

What Is Becoming Permanent?

My concern is that good habits, behaviors, and even spiritual disciplines can become permanent rituals done only for duty's sake, rather than emerging from a relational choice to love. It is important to realize that life and faith can become a practiced obligation—"the right thing to do"—with permanent, loveless effects.

Consider these daily examples that appear mundane: making the bed, brushing your teeth, feeding the dog, cleaning the kitchen, filing papers, practicing the violin, and exercising good study skills. Or consider religious tasks: prayer, regular church attendance, and Bible reading. If we do these things only because we are "supposed to," they will become rote, obligatory, and eventually meaningless tasks because they are disconnected from a personal, loving relationship with God.

For example, what do you teach your children about prayer? I have worked with countless children who know that the right response to a difficult situation is to pray but, when pressed, they have little or no expectation that it will actually accomplish anything. For them it is merely a forced habit, devoid of relationship, with no expectation that God is really there at the other end. If we aren't careful, these children will grow up believing that if prayer does not always change our circumstances, it does not work at all.

Instead, we need to teach prayer relationally. With God as our Father and Jesus as our older brother, prayer during hard times is asking them to be with us and strengthen us. These kinds of prayers do accomplish something. They build up our relationship with God and this spills over into other relationships and situations.

What Should We Be Practicing?

We must be committed to teaching our children (and reminding ourselves) that everything we do—whether great acts of service or mundane daily tasks—must be done out of a conscious decision to live our lives based on our love for God. It is from this personal conviction that we choose to serve our family, sacrifice personal desires for the sake of our neighbor, and steward our life well before the Lord. In teaching that all of life is lived before God, we are impressing on our children a different way of thinking, a different rationale for living that will serve them well when human motivation wanes.

My hope is that God would help us practice with our children the delight of living in relationship with him, a relationship that builds godly convictions and habits, and nurtures a godly view of life. What an excellent practice to become permanent in our homes!

CHAPTER 14

Technology and Your Child

Young people are made to live in relationship. They are social, interested in peers, and growing in independence. They are looking for connection and value in the relationships they build.

Matthew is a fourth grader with exceptional skills in navigating YouTube. In seconds he can find the historic pieces on Martin Luther for his history project, while also listening to the latest hip-hop artist, while also texting his friends and a girl he likes, as well as maintaining a running log on his Instagram account—all at the same time. When his mother walks into the room, with one click, he is swiftly able to demonstrate that he is still working on his history assignment. His mother goes back to cooking dinner, unaware that anything else is transpiring.

Technology and social media are a new stage on which to interact with peer groups. A new wave of teens are swiftly getting caught up in it. It is a movement that offers an effective, streamlined approach to relating with their peers. It provides enjoyment and a world of information at their fingertips and provides a form of connection. It can offer support and community for those who are isolated or lacking a link to the outside world. It connects people who share common interests, hobbies, struggles, needs, or causes.

However, it is a wave that can also sweep away a child or teen who lacks an awareness of its strength, direction, or dangers.

Technology can be used in ways that are positive and productive, but it also has the potential for fostering responses such as:

- A felt need to always be connected. It fosters a fear/anxiety of "missing out" (FOMO) on something that's going on.
- A desire to create and re-create oneself in an on-line persona.
- An unguarded freedom to express oneself and one's emotions while behind the perceived safety of an electronic screen.
- A lack of discretion in what personal information is posted publicly.
- A false sense of personal security, since everything is both permanent and public once it is put online.
- Online bullying, sexting, and pornography use.
- Addictive dependence, resulting in loss of sleep, time, and other interests.
- The risk of victimization, as grooming and predatory online behavior increases.

What Parents Must Do

Children once had a reprieve from the influence of their peers when they came home at night and talked with their parents, spent time with their siblings (of varying ages) or had solitary time. Now, the influence of peers seeps into every waking moment of their day. This lessens the strength of parental and family influence. It is this reality that should give us pause.

Wise parenting requires understanding the strong and powerful influence, budding dangers, conceivable blessings, and possible opportunities that social media brings with it. It then requires our commitment to explain these realities to our kids and to help them grow in wisdom as they get involved with this new medium.

Parents need to be willing to be educated on the issues in order to educate their family. This requires an ongoing conversation as you check in with your children and draw out their experiences online. Parents will need to be ready to discuss difficult subjects and to re-educate themselves and evaluate their practices as their children mature. It is far better to shape the way a child understands a subject than it is to try to debunk an inaccurate view.

Begin talking to children and teens early on to shape the way they understand the world of technology, its benefits and potential dangers. It is never too early to encourage godly views and establish the wise use of technology. Likewise, it is never too late. However, much heartache can be avoided when parents proactively shape their child's perspectives.

We want our children to grow up with a desire to honor God in every facet of their lives, including social media. That requires thoughtful conversations, healthy parameters, and connecting actions and consequences.

Stewardship and Accountability: Actively Monitor Your Child's Online Activities

There is a false sense of security when kids hide behind an electronic screen in the comfort of their own home. Teens assume that they are safe and alone. They think that no one can see them or know what they are doing. Sometimes they feel emboldened to say or do things they never would do in public. A young child can be playing an online game, talking to (someone they believe to be) a peer, and be lured into sharing personal information and details. Despite the many times I have heard adults say that they have talked to their kids about this, we consistently see naïve children lulled into thinking that their online contact is a harmless, trustworthy friend, even though they know nothing of the person.

It is a parent's responsibility to be sure that they actually are safe. Until young people have the maturity, tools, and skill to protect themselves, it is a parent's job to do it for them. Doing this will not be met with your child's appreciation and enthusiasm.

They will feel that you are unreasonable, a "helicopter parent," the "only parent who does this," and so on, but do not be deterred. Kids who have grown up safe should (to some degree) find it hard to believe the realities of evil you are attempting to guard them from. You may be accused of being overprotective and disregarding their privacy. Do it anyway. Stay on top of their activities.

Just as you teach a child to handle a stove, ride a bike, drive a car, or embark on any other privilege and liberty, you must also prepare them for technology and social media. We would never let a young child simply turn on a stovetop and begin playing with it, nor would we hand a fourteen-year-old the keys to a truck and expect them to have the knowledge, skill, and good judgment to drive it. We want to proactively shape the way our kids understand technology and give them the skills to steward it well.

This means that you must have a working knowledge of social media. Parents, youth workers, and counselors do not have the luxury of dismissing their ignorance as unimportant. What may not be of interest or value to you must become so for the sake of your children's well-being. When you are well educated about social media, you win the respect (and ears) of your children. You also avoid overreacting and establishing unreasonable restrictions.

Teach online safety skills. For example, personal information should never be requested or given out. Be aware of all sites and passwords your child visits or uses and check on them regularly. Even if you trust your child's online activity, there are others online with your son or daughter who are not trustworthy.

Role-play uncomfortable situations until kids can articulate what is wrong and how they would handle themselves. Give "what if" questions to prepare them for the unexpected. "What if someone asked for personal information?" "What if you got a text from someone you didn't know? What would you do?" "What if your girlfriend/ boyfriend sent you an inappropriate picture?" Make it an ongoing conversation, one that does not instill fear, but preparedness.

Children and teens are growing up in a world that thrives on technology, and we must be faithful to help them engage with it. As with many things, technology can be a useful tool and a source of enjoyment, connection, and education. It can also become an addiction, idol, or tool for malice. The more we build strong character in our children, and actively teach them to steward technology, the more likely they are to ride the wave with skill and wisdom.

CHAPTER 15

When Your Child Breaks Your Heart

Imagine getting a phone call from a police officer, informing you that your son has been caught dealing drugs in school or that your daughter caused a serious car accident with her deliberate mischief or alarming recklessness. Perhaps you'd already seen the pattern and you anticipated the day when such a call would come. You are not caught off guard. Nonetheless, it hits you like a ton of bricks. The aftereffects of your children's actions will have grave implications for their lives, and likely for yours as well.

Or perhaps you have been caught completely off guard by your "good" child's very poor conduct. Jordan's parents had always been proud of their mature, compliant daughter. She was responsible, easygoing, tenderhearted, and self-motivated. They'd brag to others, "She's the one we never have to worry about, the one we can count on." But then they received a call from the school guidance counselor, summoning them to a meeting at the high school. Jordan had written a note to a friend saying that she was pregnant and uncertain who the father was.

Even if your life circumstances do not duplicate these stories, as a parent, you likely know how these parents felt. Parents feel a deep sadness when their child has said or done something with great negative repercussions. Events like these shake you to the core. There are many ways that your child may cause you heartbreak or sorrow.

- It may be a one-time event or poor choice that now has serious, lasting implications.
- It could be a habitual pattern of sinful choices that grieve you as you watch them unfold in their lives.
- Perhaps you see the trajectory of your child's life and your heart breaks for what seems to lie ahead.
- Maybe it is the hardness of heart and relational brokenness that *you* are experiencing with them. This is a heartbreak specifically directed at you.
- It may be that the expectations you placed on your children are ones they were unable or unwilling to accept for themselves. In your honest moments, you can see that the children may not have made poor choices, but simply decisions that thwart the dreams or expectations you had for them.

Responding to Heartbreak

As a parent, you might experience a range of emotions: surprise, devastation, grief, hopelessness, helplessness, or despair. You may feel anger or shame that propels you to judge and condemn your child. How has your child broken your heart? Can you identify what you have found to be so unfathomable or painful? If you are a caring parent, you will experience the heartbreak and discouragement of your child's struggles. The key is how we choose to understand it and respond to it.

It is tempting to respond in a variety of ways. Almost certainly, you question your parenting. Did you somehow fail? Is this why your child is in this place? Did you ever really know your child as you thought you did? Were you ever on top of what was going on in his or her life? What clues did you miss? How were you so deceived? You look back over every parenting choice you ever made and wonder if you could have changed the outcome. You convince yourself that if you had been somehow different or better as a parent, this never would have occurred. The "what ifs" and "if onlys" haunt you and threaten to swallow you in despondency. You have convinced yourself that your guilt is the reason for your child's failure.

There is a place to evaluate whether our parenting mistakes have contributed to a child's struggle. It is helpful to consider whether we have been a hindrance to our children's well-being or if we failed to do something that could have spared them such trouble. But it is never beneficial to fall into a self-loathing that paralyzes. (Nor is it helpful to cling to unrealistic hopes or expectations, believing that if the child is just granted a moment of grace or insight, all turn around.) Godly sorrow leads to an honest acceptance of our responsibility and our need for repentance (2 Corinthians 7:10). It leads you to walk alongside your child toward the grace and mercy of Christ that you both need. When we as parents have a godly awareness of responsibility, it leads us to love, to offer forgiveness and to seek it, to accept blame when it is ours, and build bridges with our struggling child.

Heartbreak can humble everyone involved. It can remind us where our confidence should reside. As parents, our hearts can take a child's success or failure and treat it as our own. We can become conceited or despairing, depending on our child's performance.

But we must be careful not to tie our sense of success or failure to our children's behavior and choices. Yes, we do have tremendous influence and impact on our children. We do influence much of how they think, perceive, and respond to life. However, as we've noted previously, they are not blank slates. They are moral responders who decide for themselves whom they will serve. They come with their own strengths, weaknesses, and dispositions toward sin. They will struggle with sin, failure, and poor decisions that may have lasting ramifications.

When troubles occur, some parents experience shame. When shame enters in, they become blind to their child's struggle and the role they need to take. They are oblivious to the needs of the moment and controlled by their fears about the judgments of others. They try to hide, to cover up the failure, to silence family members from speaking about the event. They may resort to anger, rejection, or the condemnation toward anyone who threatens to expose the problem.

And it's true that if your child has a public failure, you may be judged by others. People may critique your parenting, assign blame, and think less of you or your child. But you must not be ruled by the opinions of others. Heartache is meant to humble us and point us to where our confidence as parents should rest: in the Author of our story and our child's story. We must choose not to care if others judge us and allow only the Lord to be our judge (1 Corinthians 4:3). Only God knows the heart—and that will be convicting enough! He is purifying us, reminding us to lean into him as he reveals our weakness. He is always at work in us, just as much as he is in our children. His grace is what is sufficient, not our accomplishments or our children's.

When your children's actions have heartbreaking repercussions for themselves, you, or the family, you will confront a barrage of conflicting emotions, thoughts, and reactions.

Acknowledge their impact on you. Where are you tempted to be hopeless? To give up? To abandon your child too quickly? To cut him off because it hurts too much or because it's easier than the alternative? Are you overcome with worry about the future? It's understandable to grieve the impact of what has happened, to mourn what perhaps can no longer be. But as you allow the weight of the consequences to sink in, do so remembering that God is with you in the midst of your sorrow. He has not abandoned you or your child. He specializes in bringing beauty out of ashes (Isaiah 61:3).

Take your heartbreak and allow it to deepen your trust in God. Take your child's failures and ask God to deepen his awareness of his need for Christ.

Consider Romans 8:28–36:

> And we know that for those who love God all things work together for good, for those who are called according to his purpose. . . . What then shall we say to these things? If God is for us, who can be against us? He who did not spare his own Son but gave him up for us all, how will he not also with him graciously give us all things? Who shall bring any charge against God's elect? It is God who justifies. Who is to condemn? Christ Jesus is the one who died—more than that, who was raised—who is at the right hand of God, who indeed is interceding for us. Who shall separate us from the love of Christ? Shall tribulation, or distress, or persecution, or famine, or nakedness, or danger, or sword?

Process your grief in prayer. It is tempting to forget to turn to the Lord in our troubles, or to do so only with a cry for deliverance from the consequences or for a miraculous intervention. But remember that the Spirit of the living God is within you. He will intercede on your behalf when you do not know how to pray. Do we ask God for strength and faithfulness to walk through the hardship? Do we look for God to show himself faithful to our child and to us? In our weakness, he is strong.

Acknowledge the implications for you, your family, your child—and any greater social implications. Whether the consequences feel great or small, short term or long term, wrap your arms around your children and hold them close. Allow them to see that you have not forsaken them. They need guidance. Help them navigate what to do in the midst of their sin. There is a compassion and mercy that breathes life into your children and the courage to face their consequences when they know they are not alone. You will mirror to them what a merciful God does.

Grasp Hope

"For I consider that the sufferings of this present time are not worth comparing with the glory that is to be revealed in us" (Romans 8:18). Real hope, divine hope, is not a wish. It is a certainty about God's faithfulness, a certainty that no matter what you had placed your hope in, God is up to something far better. We live not for what is seen, but for what is unseen.

Come to the Lord with confidence that he loves your family immensely. Suffering is a sign that you are sharing in the sufferings of Christ (Romans 8:7). If we share in his sufferings, we know that such heartache produces perseverance, character, and hope. Hope does not disappoint, because it is anchored in his great love for us and our children (Romans 5:3–5).

What should be our expectations of God in such circumstances? We may believe that our desires are modest, but with each simple desire comes a multitude of unspoken expectations. We have allowed our circumstances to shape our view of God, rather than allowing our confidence in God's character to shape our view of our circumstances. We are tempted to believe that God has failed us or our child. If you put your hope in anything but the Lord, it will disappoint and fail you. Hope cannot be in your child's success or good character—or your own.

Circumstances do not have the final say in a believer's life. In Scripture, we see God taking the worst of circumstances and doing the miraculous time and time again. We rarely expect too much from God; more often we expect too little. Place your hope in the character of your God and trust that he can do more than you can ask or imagine. We can have confidence in the story our Lord is writing. Allow your child's failures to deepen their awareness of their need for Christ.

Place your child's welfare above your own grief and focus on how to love your child wisely. Wrestle with your grief, acknowledge it, but don't let it drive your response. Your son or daughter needs parents who can put aside their disappointment and enter into their experience. They need their parents to show what sacrificial love looks like in the face of sin and failure. Look for ways to build bridges with them, extending grace whenever possible, and emulating Christ before them. Talk about their own sense of shame or failure; speak into any sin or hardness of heart; and faithfully walk through the aftermath with them. Your child is watching. Your children are impacted by what you choose to do with the heartbreaking decisions they've made.

God Can Redeem

A godly perspective gives you the ability to remember what is true, what is momentary, and what is eternal. It shapes what you do with your heartache and emotions and reminds you where your confidence truly lies.

Parenting includes a multitude of joys and much heartbreak. Christian homes are not immune to the trials of this world; they fall on believers and unbelievers alike. However, God promises to deliver us from the evil of it. A godly hope positions us in the center of God's will. It reminds us that we live for something better than what is temporary. It gives us a vision for eternity. That means I can trust God with my child's mistakes as well as my own.

Commit yourself to trust God in the most disheartening of circumstances, because you know that what others mean for evil God intends for good (Genesis 50:20). He who began a good work in you will be faithful to complete it (Philippians 1:6), and our hope is in the things to come (2 Corinthians 4:18).